TRAVELLERS

SWITZERLAND

By
TERESA FISHER

Written and updated by Teresa Fisher
Original photography by Christof Sonderegger

Published by Thomas Cook Publishing
A division of Thomas Cook Tour Operations Limited.
Company registration no. 3772199 England
The Thomas Cook Business Park, Unit 9, Coningsby Road,
Peterborough PE3 8SB, United Kingdom
Email: books@thomascook.com, Tel: + 44 (0) 1733 416477
www.thomascookpublishing.com

Produced by Cambridge Publishing Management Limited
Burr Elm Court, Main Street, Caldecote CB23 7NU

ISBN: 978-1-84848-149-7

First edition © 2007 Thomas Cook Publishing
This second edition © 2009
Text © Thomas Cook Publishing
Maps © Thomas Cook Publishing/PCGraphics (UK) Limited

Project Editor: Adam Royal
Series Editor: Maisie Fitzpatrick
Production/DTP: Steven Collins

Printed and bound in Italy by Printer Trento

Cover photography: Front L–R: © David Noton Photography/Alamy;
© Mediacolors/Alamy; © BL Images Ltd/Alamy. Back: © Johanna
Huber/4Corners images

Contents

Introduction

Switzerland often conjures up such clichéd images as yodelling goatherds and cows with giant cowbells set against a bucolic backdrop of flower-filled meadows, crystal-clear Alpine lakes, cosy wooden chalets and majestic snow-capped mountains. Admittedly, the country does have more than its fair share of 'chocolate-box' scenery, but there's much more to discover in this fascinating, multifaceted country than Heidi, Swatch®, cheese and chocolate.

Switzerland lies at the heart of a diverse physical and cultural European region, landlocked in the Alps and squeezed between France, Germany, Liechtenstein, Austria and Italy. Not only is the land divided into three distinct geographical areas (the Alps, the Jura mountains and a central plateau known as the Mittelland – Middle Land), but there are also four linguistic regions – German, French (called Suisse Romande), Italian and Romansh – where lifestyles and customs follow cultural and social rather than national boundaries.

Even the country's food is a delicious *mélange* of all that is best in French, Italian and German cuisine, together with ubiquitous homespun dishes like muesli and gooey cheese fondue. Yet, despite a history that has often pitted one region against another, this melting pot of traditions and customs has learned to survive as a cohesive unit in order to protect the neutrality that is its safeguard. For over 700 years, Switzerland – officially known as the Swiss Confederation – has maintained the world's oldest democracy, achieving an exceptionally high standard of living and the highest incomes per capita in the world. Indeed, Switzerland's small area and modest population give little indication of its unique character or its significance on the world scene.

Medieval buildings, Luzern

Silsersee in the Engadine, through a larch forest

The mountains are the nation's heart and soul, covering nearly two-thirds of the landscape. Thanks to the Alps, with their snowy crags, deep gorges and vast glaciers, the Swiss are extremely sports-conscious and have carefully nurtured mountaineering, hiking, skiing and other adventure sports as tourist attractions. Tourism is one of the nation's main industries; the transport infrastructure is superb (the trains are famously punctual), and Swiss hospitality is second to none. It is a land for all seasons, with exceptional hiking, biking and water sports in spring, summer and autumn; sensational skiing in winter, and a wide choice of superlative, year-round resorts, including the celebrated St Moritz, Gstaad, Interlaken, Verbier and Zermatt.

The nation has some fascinating cities, including pint-sized Bern, the capital; historic, medieval Luzern; Zurich, the largest metropolis, known for its arts, shopping and nightlife; Lugano, in the balmy, sun-drenched canton of Ticino; and cosmopolitan Geneva, located on the giant croissant-shaped Lac Léman or Lake Geneva – Switzerland's largest lake.

Although Switzerland may not rank foremost as a European cultural destination, it has the greatest density of museums and galleries, and nine UNESCO World Heritage Sites. A major global financial centre and the headquarters of over 300 international institutions, Switzerland has also produced more Nobel Prize winners than any other nation. Indeed, this extraordinary quadrilingual land cleverly combines *la dolce vita* of the Italians, the *savoir faire* of the French, and the punctuality and precision of the Germans to create a unique and versatile nation and one of Europe's favourite holiday playgrounds.

The land

Switzerland is a small, landlocked country at the heart of Europe, sharing borders with Austria, France, Germany, Italy and Liechtenstein. The nation is divided into 26 self-governing regions called 'cantons', with its capital at Bern. Most of the country's 7.5 million live in the main cities north of the Alps – Zurich, Basel, Bern, Lausanne and Geneva.

Glaciation

The Swiss countryside is split into three main geographical areas: the Alps, the Jura mountains, and the agriculturally rich central plateau or Mittelland (Middle Land), where most of the country's economic activities and cities are concentrated. Each area has been shaped largely by glaciation. Over 60 per cent of Switzerland's 41,285sq km (15,940 sq miles) are the mountain ranges of the Alps, which reach a maximum height of 4,634m (15,203ft)

at the Dufourspitze in Valais. The Ice Age also hollowed out the valleys and led to the formation of the land's many beautiful lakes which, together with the mountains, play a leading role in Switzerland's spectacular scenery.

The Alps

The Alps are one of the largest and highest mountain ranges in the world, stretching from Slovenia in the east, through Austria, Germany, Italy, Liechtenstein and Switzerland to France

The world-famous Matterhorn

in the west. The Swiss Alps are its centrepiece, representing roughly 20 per cent of the entire range, with approximately 100 peaks close to or higher than 4,000m (13,125ft) above sea level. There are also over 3,000sq km (1,158 sq miles) of glaciers. The largest is the Aletsch Gletscher in the Bernese Alps – 23.6km (14½ miles) long and covering an area of 115sq km (44 sq miles).

Although the Swiss Alps are sparsely populated, many mountain resorts have developed, with cogwheel railways and aerial cable cars providing easy access to high altitudes. Centuries ago, traversable high mountain passes (including the Grand St Bernard, Simplon and St Gotthard passes) across the Alps were constructed to link northern and southern Europe. They all now possess impressive, lengthy road and/or train tunnels through the mountains.

The mountains are the nation's main tourist attraction, especially for skiing and snow sports in winter, and for hiking, biking and climbing in summer. Some of the peaks count among the world's greatest mountaineering challenges, including the mighty Eiger and the Matterhorn, Switzerland's most famous mountain.

The Jura range in the northwest is shared with France. It dates from the Jurassic era (to which it lends its name), and occupies about 10 per cent of Switzerland. In contrast to the Alps, the Jura are low, forested and

The dam at Lac d'Emosson in Valais

undulating, but are nonetheless popular for mountain biking, hiking and cross-country skiing.

Rivers and lakes

The Alps are broken by the great valleys of the Rhône in Valais, the Rhine and the Inn in Graubünden, and the Ticino in Ticino. This central Alpine region is a major watershed of Europe, with each river draining into a different sea: the Rhine to the North Sea; the Inn to the Black Sea; and the Rhône and the Ticino (called the Po after it leaves Lake Maggiore) into the Mediterranean. Switzerland also hosts many lakes, from the large Lac Léman (from the pre-Celtic word *lem*, meaning 'large water') and Bodensee (Lake Constance) – to hundreds of tiny, crystal-clear lakes in the mountains. Some of them are dammed to provide hydroelectric power, producing over 60 per cent of the country's electricity supply. The rest of the supply is nuclear powered.

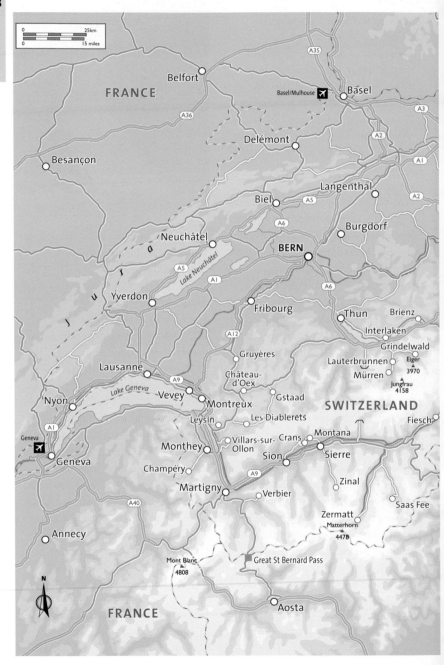

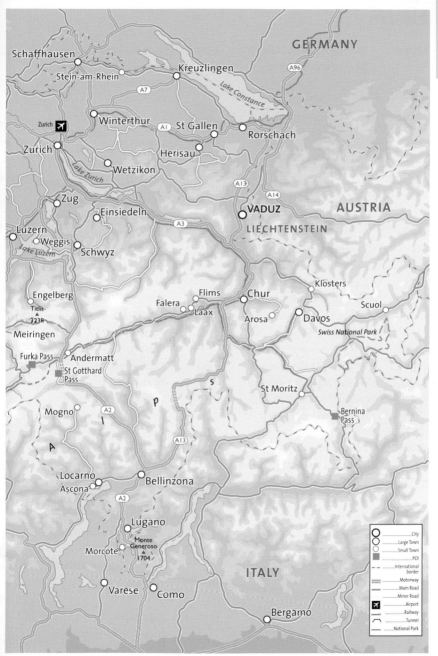

Schaffhausen
Stein-am-Rhein
GERMANY
A96
Kreuzlingen
A7
Lake Constance
Zurich ✈
Winterthur
A1
St Gallen
Rorschach
Zurich
Herisau
Lake Zurich
Wetzikon
Zug
Einsiedeln
A3
VADUZ
AUSTRIA
LIECHTENSTEIN
Luzern
Weggis
Lake Luzern
Schwyz
A13
A14
Engelberg
Titlis
2238
Falera
Flims
Chur
Klosters
Scuol
Meiringen
Laax
Arosa
Davos
Furka Pass
Andermatt
Swiss National Park
St Gotthard
Pass
S
Mogno
A2
St Moritz
p
Bernina
Pass
l
A13
A
Locarno
Bellinzona
Ascona
A2
Lugano
Monte
Generoso
Morcote
1704
ITALY
Varese
Como
Bergamo

○ City
◎ Large Town
○ Small Town
■ POI
International border
Motorway
Main Road
Minor Road
✈ Airport
Railway
Tunnel
National Park

History

| 1500 BC | Celtic Raetian and Helvetii tribes settle north of the Alps. |

| 58 BC | The Romans, under Julius Caesar, seize Helvetia and Raetia. |

| c.AD 400 | Roman legions withdraw as Germanic tribes take over the region. |

| 742 | Charlemagne (Charles the Great) absorbs the land into his Holy Roman Empire. A feudal system develops and Christian monasteries hold sway. |

| 1100s | The Dukes of Zähringen take control of the western lands and found Fribourg (1157) and Bern (1191). |

| c.1200 | The road over the St Gotthard Pass is opened and the Forest Cantons (Uri, Schwyz and Unterwalden) become reichsfrei (independent city states within the Holy Roman Empire), controlling the pass with tolls and taxes. |

| 1218 | The cities become reichsfrei at the end of the Zähringer dynasty. |

| 1273 | The Habsburg dynasty takes control of much of northern Switzerland and revokes the Reichsfreiheit. |

| 1291 | Charter of Confederation signed on the Rütli meadow. |

| 1315 | The Forest Cantons revolt against the Habsburgs. Following a famous victory at Morgarten in 1315, their union – the Swiss Confederacy – is recorded in the Federal Charter. They collectively become Schwyzers and the nation is dubbed Schwyz. |

| 1353 | The cantons of Glarus and Zug and the city states of Luzern, Zurich and Bern join the Confederation. |

| 1481 | Fribourg and Solothurn join the Confederation. |

| 1499 | The Swabian War brings Swiss independence from the Holy Roman Empire. Basel and Schaffhausen join the Confederation in 1501. |

| 1506 | Pope Julius II engages the Swiss Guard, which still serves the Vatican today. |

1513 The two Appenzeller half-cantons join the Confederation.

1523 Priest Huldrych Zwingli's Protestant Reformation is adopted by Zurich and half the cantons. The others remain staunchly Catholic.

1798 Switzerland is overrun by the French and becomes a battlefield during the French Revolutionary Wars.

1803 Napoleon's Act of Mediation restores partial sovereignty, and Aargau, Graubünden, St Gallen, Thurgau, Ticino and Vaud cantons join the Confederation.

1815 The Congress of Vienna re-establishes Swiss independence and declares Switzerland's neutrality. Geneva, Neuchâtel and Valais become officially recognised cantons, and Switzerland gets its final boundaries.

1847 The Sonderbundskrieg (between Catholic and Protestant cantons) is the last armed conflict on Swiss territory, and results in the formation of the Federal Constitution of 1848.

1864 The International Red Cross is founded in Geneva.

1914 Switzerland remains neutral during World Wars I and II.

1920 Switzerland joins the League of Nations.

1963 Switzerland joins the Council of Europe.

1979 The Jura separates from the canton of Bern, forming Switzerland's youngest canton.

1992 Swiss people vote against joining the EEA (European Economic Area).

2002 Switzerland votes to join the United Nations (UN).

2003 Swiss sailing team Alinghi wins the America's Cup. Basel-born tennis player Roger Federer wins the first of five consecutive titles at Wimbledon.

2005 Switzerland signs the Schengen treaty, showing their European Union (EU) support.

2008 Switzerland co-hosts the Union of European Football Associations Championships with Austria.

William Tell

The legend

According to legend, Wilhelm Tell (William Tell) was a simple peasant, hunter and family man who came from the village of Bürglen in the Uri canton. In November 1307, he allegedly travelled to Altdorf, capital of the Uri canton. As he crossed the town square, he chose to ignore the hat of the tyrannical Habsburg bailiff named Gessler. This hat had been placed on a pole to represent his imperial authority, and locals were expected to bow before it as a sign of reverence or face charges of treason. Tell was arrested and Gessler threatened to execute him unless he could prove his skill as a marksman. He placed an apple on the head of Tell's son, Walter, and ordered him to shoot it off. If he missed, both would die. The bolt from Tell's crossbow split the apple in two. He then confessed to having a second arrow for Gessler should his son have been injured,

The Telldenkmal in Altdorf

DID WILLIAM TELL EVER EXIST?

Over the years, Tell has become a hero symbolising the struggle for political and individual freedom, inextricably linked with the founding of the Swiss Confederation. Many Swiss people still believe that he once existed. His classic tale is told by Gilg Tschudi in the highly regarded *Chronicon Helveticum* (published in 1734–36). However, there is no mention of William Tell either in the Habsburg state archives in Vienna or in any of Uri's historical records. The stirring story of patriotism attained worldwide renown in 1804 through the play *Wilhelm Tell* by German dramatist Friedrich von Schiller, and again in 1829 in the opera *Guillaume Tell* by Gioacchino Rossini. The William Tell overture remains one of Rossini's best-known compositions today.

and so the wicked overlord refused to free him, putting him on a boat heading for jail in Küssnacht. During the voyage, a sudden storm blew up and Tell was released to steer the boat to safety, because of his knowledge of the Vierwaldstättersee (Lake of the Four Cantons). Tell leapt ashore near Sisikon and managed to escape by pushing the boat and its crew back out into the stormy lake. He ambushed Gessler's party in the forest en route to Küssnacht, and shot the tyrant through the heart with his last arrow.

'Tell' tourism

William Tell has long been considered part of the national identity and a symbol of Swiss culture. There is a handful of low-key 'Tell' tourist sights in and around the canton of Uri. These include the Tellsplatte, the flat rock where Tell jumped ashore from his boat near Sisikon, and the nearby Tellskapelle (Tell Chapel) with beautiful frescoes depicting his story. The church in Bürglen, Tell's home village, also has interior frescoes portraying the legend, a commemorative Tellbrunnen (Tell Fountain) and a Tellmuseum (*www.tellmuseum.ch*). A Telldenkmal (Tell Monument) stands in Altdorf's main square, where the apple shooting reputedly occurred, and the Tell Spielhaus (Playhouse,

The statue of William Tell by Lake Lugano

www.theater-uri.ch) here occasionally stages topical dramas. The William Tell Express is a one-day excursion (*www.wilhelmtellexpress.ch*) from Luzern by boat across the Vierwaldstättersee to Flüelen, then by panoramic train southwards through the Gotthard tunnel and down through Ticino to Locarno.

Politics

The political organisation of Switzerland is unique and complex, functioning on both federal and cantonal levels. The autonomous cantons were first formed into a modern federal state in 1848 – a decentralised system, relying on the solidarity of the individual 26 cantons for peaceful coexistence. The federal authorities have the most political power, representing the interests of the nation abroad, and ensuring each canton is given equal consideration in domestic issues.

Direct democracy

Switzerland's voting system is unique among modern democratic nations. Its political system is not based on the usual confrontation between the party in power and its opposition, but rather it is dependent upon general consensus, giving the ultimate power to the people by means of 'direct democracy'. Any Swiss citizen over 18 years old can vote and stand for election. The people elect their own parliamentary representatives and, four times a year, the entire nation votes on a variety of federal, cantonal and municipal issues. The people can also have their say by popular ballot, or by referendum, to veto proposed laws. If a citizen can gather 50,000 signatures against the law within 100 days, a national vote has to be scheduled in which the people determine the outcome by simple majority.

The Swiss parliament building, Bundeshaus

The United Nations office in Geneva

Parliament

The Swiss parliament, based in Bern, is made up of two chambers of equal standing – the National Council and the Council of States – with seats allocated by proportional representation and by canton size. Members are not full-time politicians and they only convene for three four-week sessions annually. The cabinet (or Federal Council) has seven members, and since 2004 consists of two members from each of the main parties – the SVP (Swiss People's Party), SPS (Social Democratic Party) and the FDP (Free Democratic Party) – and one member from the CVP (Christian Democratic Party).

Foreign relations

Neutral Switzerland has traditionally avoided any alliances potentially entailing military or political action. However, it joined the Council of Europe in 1963 and the United Nations in 2002 as a result of a popular vote. It is also home to many international organisations including the World Health Organization (WHO) and the International Red Cross (whose flag is the Swiss flag with the colours reversed). Over the years, it has hosted many major international treaty conferences, thereby playing a pivotal role in world peace. Switzerland is not a member of the EU, but in 2005 it joined the Schengen treaty and Dublin Convention, again by popular vote – a shrewd move, giving the nation all the EU benefits but few of the commitments.

WOMEN'S RIGHTS

One of the most celebrated moments of Swiss political history was in 1971 when women were finally granted a federal vote. Thereafter, women were slowly given a cantonal vote, except in Appenzell Innerrhoden where in 1990 the Federal Court had to intervene. Together with Glarus, Innerrhoden is also the last canton to use the ancient *Landsgemeinde* system of direct democracy. Rather than ballot or postal voting, the citizens gather in traditional dress in Appenzell's main square on the last Sunday in April, and respond to a series of shouted questions by voting with daggers.

Culture

Switzerland is a country of many contradictions: politically conservative yet culturally innovative and artistically liberal. With its four language groups and diversity of landscapes and lifestyles, the country has nurtured both a tradition-rich culture in rural areas – where people still wear folk costumes during festivals and preserve their traditional music and folklore – and a highly creative, forward-looking approach to culture in the cities.

Art and architecture

Switzerland's thriving art scene has long attracted global attention. Some of the most important figures in 20th-century art are Swiss, including the expressionist artist, Paul Klee; Alberto Giacometti, famous for his elongated human sculptures; Jean Tinguely, with his bizarre mechanistic scrap-metal sculptures; and Max Bill, who developed and popularised 'concrete' art (as opposed to 'abstract') in the 1950s.

According to Switzerland Tourism, 'there is a gallery worth visiting every 30km (18 miles) between Geneva and St Gallen', with top venues including Zurich's Kunsthaus, Basel's Kunstmuseum, the Musée d'Art et d'Histoire in Geneva, Sammlung Rosengart in Luzern, Zentrum Paul Klee in Bern, and Winterthur's Oskar Reinhart collections.

Switzerland has also played a pivotal role in architecture, from its beautifully preserved medieval UNESCO treasures such as Bern city centre and the three fortresses of Bellinzona, through to the new modernist designs by local architects (*see pp56–7*).

Literature

Many foreign writers have visited or moved to Switzerland, including Voltaire, Victor Hugo, Ernest

Museum of Jean Tinguely's art, Basel

DADA

The deliberately nonsensical Dada art movement was founded in Zurich in 1916 by wartime exiles, such as Hans Arp, Hugo Ball and Tristan Tzara, as a cultural reaction to the war. A rebellious new 'anti-art', Dadaism reached its peak in 1920. Years later, even Dada artists described the movement as 'nihilistic … a systematic work of destruction and demoralisation … embracing anarchy and the irrational.' (*Gardner's Art Through the Ages*, Fred Kleiner and Christin Mamiya, 2005).

If you like classical music, there are performances throughout the year in most cities

Hemingway and Graham Greene, and have written books set in the country. Lord Byron's celebrated *The Prisoner of Chillon* was based on Lake Geneva's Château de Chillon, and Arthur Conan Doyle's famous character Sherlock Holmes fell to his death at the Reichenbach Falls near Meiringen. Swiss writers are less well known, and Johanna Spyri's celebrated *Heidi* (*see p105*) remains the most famous Swiss novel of all times. Other celebrated Swiss authors include Henri Rousseau, Madame de Staël and Swiss-German Hermann Hesse. Among the masters of Germanic literature count Zurich-born Max Frisch (1911–91) with his dark, Kafkaesque writings; detective fiction writer, Friedrich Dürrenmatt (1921–90); and Gottfried Keller (1819–90), whose *Green Henry* is set in Zurich.

Music and theatre

Switzerland has musical entertainment to suit all tastes, from highbrow classical concerts to yodelling and alphorn quartets. There is a symphony orchestra in every main city, and there are concerts and music festivals throughout the year. Two of the most renowned are the Luzern Festival and the Montreux International Jazz Festival.

Most Swiss theatre is in French, German or Italian, and therefore not usually very appealing to visitors, although the entertaining puppet theatre productions generally require little or no linguistic knowledge. Switzerland's largest theatre is the Schauspielhaus in Zurich, one of the most prestigious theatres in the German-speaking world. Zurich stages world-class opera in the Opernhaus from September to May, and the celebrated Béjart Ballet company in Lausanne is always booked for months in advance.

Festivals and events

Switzerland's well-organised programme of events and festivals span the calendar from New Year and Carnival to Christmas, and attract visitors from around the world. They range from ski races and jazz festivals to rather more traditional, quirky occasions such as the annual yodelling festival, onion market and decorated cow processions. Unless specified, the events mentioned here fall on different dates each year. Contact the local tourist offices for further details.

January

13, 20 or 27 – Vogel Gryff Volksfest (Feast of the Griffin), Basel. A griffin, lion and 'wild man' (representing the three main neighbourhoods of the city) float down the River Rhine on a raft, followed by street parades and parties.

Inferno Race Mürren. At 15.8km (9³/4 miles), the world's longest amateur ski race (*see p107*).

International Hot Air Ballooning Week Chateau-d-Oex.

Polo World Cup on Snow St Moritz.

World Cup, Olympia Bob Run St Moritz.

February

Fasnacht (Carnival) celebrations throughout Switzerland (prior to Lent). Basel claims the most flamboyant fancy-dress parades, street entertainment and fireworks. In Bern, a 'bear' is awakened from hibernation in the Prison Tower with the Ychüblete, a spectacular parade of drums.

Velogemel (Snow Bike) World Championships Grindelwald.

White Turf International horse racing on ice, St Moritz.

March

Engadine Ski Marathon 42km (26 miles) from Maloja to Zuoz.

Geneva International Motor Show

April

Alpauffahrt Decorative cow processions, in rural areas (*see p96*).

International Zurich Marathon Switzerland's largest marathon.

Primavera Concertistica (Spring Festival of Concerts), Locarno.

Sechseläuten (Six o'clock Chimes). Zurich's Spring Festival features a procession of the city's guilds on horseback and the ignition of the *Böög* (a snowman-like figure made of straw and fireworks who represents winter) at 6pm. The faster his head explodes, the better the summer will be!

May
Corpus Christi Solemn processions in Catholic towns and regions.

June
Bol d'Or Race International Sailing Regatta on Lake Geneva.
Jazz Ascona New Orleans jazz features on six stages by the idyllic waterfront (*until mid-July*).
Tellspiele Interlaken. Open-air performances of Schiller's famous *William Tell* play (*until mid-Sept*).
Yodelling Festival Northeast Switzerland's annual event, St Moritz.
Zurich Festival Major international music, opera, theatre and cultural festival (*until end July*).

July
Montreux International Jazz Festival The world's most prestigious jazz festival.

August
Festival Internazionale del Film Locarno's film festival.
Fêtes de Genève Two weeks of flower parades, fireworks and live music events.
Luzern Festival Concerts, theatre and art exhibitions (*until mid-Sept*).
Settimane Musicali Ascona. International classical music festival (*until mid-Oct*).
Zurich Street Parade This colourful techno street parade, drawing over one million partygoers, is Europe's largest annual street party, with dancing day and night.

September
Alpabfahrt Seasonal cow processions (*see p96*).
Jungfrau Marathon 42km (26 miles) from Brienz to the Eiger, with an altitude difference of 1,810m (5,938ft) – Europe's toughest race.

October
Älpler Chilbi Local Unterwalden festival to celebrate the end of the Alpine summer, with traditional costume and a procession of cowbells.
Wine Growers' Festival Lugano.

November
Zibelemärit Bern. Traditional Onion Market and folk festival (*fourth Monday in Nov*).

December
Christmas markets throughout the country. Basel boasts the largest, most traditional market, featuring arts and crafts from all over Switzerland.
6 Dec – St Nicholas Parade. St Nicholas visits Fribourg on the back of a donkey, and distributes sweets and gingerbread to the local children.
12 Dec – L'Escalade, Geneva. Three days and nights of non-stop processions, period costumes, folk music, banquets and fireworks celebrating Geneva's independence.
31 Dec – Silvester. Zurich hosts the nation's largest annual New Year's Eve party; Urnäsch in Appenzellerland celebrates twice (on 31 Dec and on 13 Jan, in keeping with the Julian calendar).

Outdoor activities

The Swiss countryside is a giant open-air recreation area with activities to suit all ages and abilities. The mountains are among the most challenging and spectacular in all of Europe, but you don't have to be a mountaineer or a skier (*see p106*) to enjoy them. Switzerland offers some of Europe's finest walking, and a host of other outdoor activities.

Mountain activities

With over 60,000km (37,300 miles) of marked trails, Switzerland has sensational hiking opportunities to suit all ages and levels of fitness, with easy access to upper slopes and otherwise remote paths through a comprehensive network of mountain railways, gondolas and chairlifts. Contact the Swiss Hiking Federation for further information (*www.swisshiking.ch*).

Cycling is also a popular pastime, ranging from day-to-day cycle routes in the cities, to weekend mountain-bike tours over Alpine passes and the Tour de Suisse (*www.tds.ch*) in June. Many cities, including Zurich, Bern, Geneva and Lausanne, offer free bike hire for up to two hours from May to October (*www.schweizrollt.ch*), and

there are nine national long-distance bike routes spanning the country, offering 3,300km (2,000 miles) of signed paths, mostly away from traffic (*www.cycling-in-switzerland.ch*). It is easy to rent a bike, and tourist offices can provide cycle maps.

Inline-skating is popular too, especially along the promenades of lakes Zurich and Geneva, and on the nation's three long-distance skating routes, each around 200km (124 miles). Ice-skating is a beloved winter activity, with natural ice rinks in most resorts, together with sleigh rides, snowshoe hikes, spas and curling for non-skiers. Ice hockey is a major spectator sport with a keenly contested national league.

During summer months, horse riding and golf are popular pursuits. Most golf courses welcome visitors (see *www.asg.ch* for information), although only a handful open all year round. In St Moritz, golf is played on the snow in winter, with orange balls and greens called 'whites'. The nation's latest craze is swing-golf; this is played on unprepared terrain with a soft ball and a special three-sided club.

Soak up the scenery from your saddle

Water sports

The Swiss love swimming, especially at the lakeside lidos of Zurich and Geneva during summer, and in open-air thermal pools in winter. Fishing is popular in the various lakes and rivers (contact the local tourist office for advice on obtaining a licence). Most major lakes hire boats to visitors ranging from small motor craft to pedalos. Lakes Thun, Maggiore, Geneva and Zurich are major sailing venues, while Rotsee near Luzern is the rowing capital. Windsurfing, wakeboarding and kitesurfing are especially popular at Silvaplana, near St Moritz, and canoeing and white-water rafting in the Bernese Oberland are guaranteed to get your adrenalin flowing.

Adrenalin activities

Switzerland is the world's second-largest adventure sports destination, after New Zealand. Rock climbing (and climbing frozen waterfalls) is as popular as ever in mountainous regions, while *via ferrata* – specially developed metal ladders embedded into steep rock faces – facilitate climbing without ropes, to allow both experienced and more novice climbers and hikers to reach the summits.

Other extreme activities include canyoning, bungee jumping, zorbing (rolling downhill strapped inside a giant plastic sphere), hydrospeeding (river surfing), paragliding, hang-gliding and heli-skiing. Yet it's hard to beat the Bob and Cresta Runs at St Moritz (see *p109*) for the ultimate adrenalin rush.

Highlights

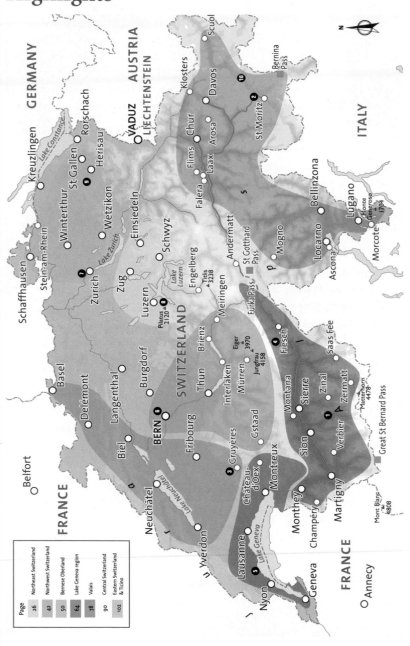

GERMANY

AUSTRIA

LIECHTENSTEIN

VADUZ

ITALY

FRANCE

FRANCE

SWITZERLAND

BERN

Scuol

Klosters

Davos

Bernina Pass

St Moritz

Arosa

Chur

Flims

Laax

Falera

Bellinzona

Lugano

Monte Generoso 1704

Morcote

Locarno

Ascona

Mogno

Andermatt

St Gotthard Pass

Furka Pass

Rorschach

Kreuzlingen

Lake Constance

St Gallen

Herisau

Winterthur

Wetzikon

Einsiedeln

Schwyz

Engelberg

Titlis 3238

Meiringen

Fiesch

Saas Fee

Zermatt

Matterhorn 4478

Great St Bernard Pass

Schaffhausen

Stein-am-Rhein

Lake Zurich

Zurich

Zug

Luzern

Pilatus 2120

Lake Luzern

Brienz

Thun

Interlaken

Mürren

Eiger 3970

Jungfrau 4158

Montana

Sierre

Zinal

Sion

Verbier

Martigny

Mont Blanc 4808

Basel

Delémont

Langenthal

Burgdorf

Biel

Fribourg

Gruyères

Gstaad

Châteaud'Oex

Montreux

Monthey

Champéry

Belfort

Neuchâtel

Lake Neuchâtel

Yverdon

Lausanne

Lake Geneva

Nyon

Geneva

Annecy

1 **Skiing or snowboarding in the canton of Valais** 'Chocolate-box' chalet villages, rugged mountain scenery and the Matterhorn as a backdrop (*see p78*).

2 **Travelling by train through breathtaking Alpine scenery on the *Glacier Express*** One of Europe's greatest rail journeys (*see p110*).

3 **Visiting Gruyères** Home to Switzerland's famous cheese and one of the most photogenic villages in Switzerland (*see p46*).

4 **Marvelling at the 23.6km (14½-mile) long Aletsch Gletscher** The largest glacier in Europe and the highlight of the Jungfrau-Aletsch-Bietschhorn UNESCO World Natural Heritage Site (*see p82*).

5 **Exploring the Swiss Riviera** Glamorous resorts, castles and vineyards on the slopes of Lake Geneva (*see p64*).

6 **Admiring Switzerland's beautiful and fascinating capital, Bern** On the banks of the River Aare, Bern has an atmospheric medieval, arcaded Altstadt (Old Town) (*see p54*).

7 **Window-shopping in Zurich** To suit all tastes and budgets, from the tiny boutiques and quirky specialist stores of the Niederdorf to the watches, jewellery, chocolates and haute couture of the world-famous shopping mile, the Bahnhofstrasse (*see p30*).

8 **Hiking in William Tell country** Around Luzern, Pilatus and the Vierwaldstättersee (Lake of the Four Cantons), this area has a remarkable blend of lakes, mountains, history, culture and folklore, all steeped in the history of the formation of Switzerland (*see p90*).

9 **Exploring rustic Appenzell** The most traditional of cantons, with its verdant, rolling landscapes, slow pace of life and beautiful villages of ornately painted houses, almost untouched by modern times (*see p36*).

10 **Enjoying the Engadine** One of the most spectacular mountain regions, offering a multitude of activities including skiing in glitzy St Moritz, hiking in Switzerland's only national park or relaxing in the spa baths of charming Scuol (*see p108*).

Suggested itineraries

Long weekend

Visitors are spoilt for choice when visiting Switzerland for a long weekend. City breaks are increasingly popular, and Zurich is hard to beat for sightseeing, shopping and nightlife. The city centre is compact and easy to explore on foot. Explore the car-free Altstadt (Old Town) with its graceful spires and cobbled alleyways, and the ancient quarter of Niederdorf fringing the river. Then visit the Kunsthaus (Museum of Fine Arts), the nation's top gallery, and the Schweizerisches Landesmuseum (Swiss National Museum) for a fascinating overview of the nation. If you don't have time for a boat trip on Zurichsee (Lake Zurich), join the locals promenading on its eastern shore. You can shop in the celebrated designer boutiques of Bahnhofstrasse; taste the world's finest chocolates at Sprüngli in Paradeplatz; and experience the nation's best nightlife – from world-class opera and theatre to mellow jazz bars, raucous beer cellars, sophisticated cocktail bars and trendy nightclubs.

If a city break doesn't appeal, head to Appenzellerland for a taste of Switzerland at its most charmingly stereotypical. Here, in this beautiful, sleepy canton you will find locals dressed in traditional costume, quaint villages of painted wooden houses, folkloric museums, meadows of wild flowers, cows with giant cowbells, and you may even hear some yodelling. The highest peak in the region, Säntis, affords spectacular views over eastern Switzerland.

In winter months, a ski weekend is a viable option, thanks to the nation's superb rail network, with quick and easy access to the resorts. Flims, Laax and Klosters are within two hours by train from Zurich, while Les Diablerets and the resorts of the Alpes Vaudoìses are between a 90-minute and two-hour drive from Geneva.

One week

A week gives you sufficient time to visit some of the most popular cities in both the French- and German-speaking regions. Spend just two days in Zurich (*see above*) then take the train to Luzern for two days, to explore the medieval Altstadt, to stroll beside the lake and to visit the famous Sammlung Rosengart and the Verkehrshaus der Schweiz (Swiss Transport Museum). Luzern is ideally situated for excursions into the surrounding 'William Tell Country', so spend your second day on a nostalgic paddle-steamer excursion visiting the traditional villages of the Vierwaldstättersee (Lake of the Four Cantons), or combine this with the world's steepest cogwheel railway to the top of majestic Mount Pilatus for vistas of central Switzerland's exceptional Alpine scenery.

Continue by train to spend a day admiring the beautifully preserved medieval architecture of the capital city, Bern. On the fringes of town, the Zentrum Paul Klee is a must for art aficionados. End your week travelling by train along the Swiss Riviera to the gracious city of Geneva, to see the cobbled Vieille Ville (Old Town), with its impressive cathedral, the beautiful gardens, the lake and the fascinating Musée International de la Croix-Rouge et du Croissant-Rouge (Red Cross and Red Crescent Museum).

Two weeks

An extra week will enable you to do the one-week itinerary (*see opposite*), and to add a tour (by car or train) of the Swiss Riviera, the Bernese Oberland and Gruyères. Lac Léman (Lake Geneva) is the nation's largest lake and one of the most beautiful. Stroll amid the Lavaux vineyards that swathe the northern slopes of the lake, and taste their produce in the tiny, ancient wine villages that dot the landscape. Take a cruise along the shores to visit Château de Chillon, with its foundations dipping into the lake, and the sophisticated *Belle Époque* resorts of Vevey and Montreux which, for centuries, have drawn the rich and famous to their shores.

Head north through the lush pre-Alpine countryside of Fribourgerland to visit the famed village of Gruyères, with its perfectly preserved medieval houses, and fairy-tale castle. Then continue on to the Bernese Oberland to see the astonishing Aletsch Gletscher,

the longest glacier in western Eurasia; historic Interlaken, the home of tourism; and the region's world-famous mountains – the Eiger, Mönch and Jungfrau. The train ride to the Jungfrau's summit is a sensational day out.

Longer

A longer stay allows you to travel to remoter regions deep in the Swiss countryside. It also provides time in your busy schedule to have a fondue, buy some souvenirs and eat some more chocolate.

Depending on the season, skiing or hiking in Valais is a must. The winter resorts here, including Verbier and Zermatt, offer some of the most challenging skiing and liveliest après-ski in the Alps. The canton also boasts more 4,000m (13,124ft) peaks than anywhere in Switzerland, ensuring dazzling Alpine vistas at every turn. The Engadine is another beautiful region to explore, wild and unkempt and easily accessible from Valais, via the *Glacier Express* train from Zermatt to the ultimate winter playground of St Moritz.

Herdsmen at a cattle show in Appenzellerland

Northeast Switzerland

Although not a region of high alps, northeast Switzerland contains some of the most breathtaking scenery, including Lake Constance and Appenzellerland; some of the prettiest medieval villages, including Schaffhausen and Stein-am-Rhein; internationally renowned art galleries in Zurich and Winterthur; and Zurich itself – the nation's most stylish city.

For many, Zurich is simply a gateway for those flying to the Alps. For others, it is considered a dull, cold-hearted banking city. Yet today's Zurich is Switzerland's largest city – a dynamic and thriving metropolis, large enough to offer world-class facilities but small enough to retain its Swiss charm and 19th-century intimacy. Switzerland's finest museums include Zurich's Kunsthaus (Museum of Fine Arts) and the Schweizerisches Landesmuseum (Swiss National Museum); it also boasts the nation's most celebrated boutiques

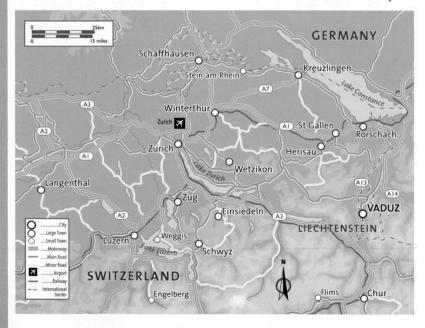

You can visit the villages around Lake Constance by boat

– known for their extravagant designer clothes, watches, jewellery and chocolates – and the magnificent Lake Zurich for recreation.

Bodensee (Lake Constance) is the other major lake in the region, and it is a hugely popular holiday destination due to the string of genteel towns, picturesque villages and pleasant beaches that lines its shores – it is often referred to as the 'German Riviera'. South of Lake Constance, the residents of Appenzellerland are often the butt of Swiss jokes, mocked for their folksy ways. However, for visitors this is a wonderfully rustic region of exceptional beauty and charm. Its villages remain virtually untouched by modern times, and the conservative locals cherish their rural customs, traditional costumes and slow pace of life. If anywhere represents stereotypical Switzerland, it is Appenzellerland.

Zurich

Zurich may not be the political capital, but it is Switzerland's spiritual one due to its vibrant art and music scene, the most luxurious shopping in Europe, and the infectious *joie de vivre* of its people. Gone is the old image of a cold, characterless financial city of staid bankers and precision timing – this is the fourth-largest financial centre in the world (after New York, London and Tokyo). Zurich is now a stylish city that cleverly combines its impressive architectural and cultural heritage with cutting-edge innovations in fashion and design. As with all Swiss cities, everything runs like clockwork and everywhere is spotlessly clean, but Zurich is nonetheless a fun-loving city. The Zurichers work hard, but they certainly also know how to play hard and, for seven years running, Zurich has been voted the number one place to live in the world (Quality of Living ranking published by consulting group Mercer).

Zurich is a stunningly beautiful city with more than its fair share of picturesque buildings flanking the River Limmat. The river flows into Lake Zurich, the fourth-largest lake in Switzerland, with its beautiful grassy parks, promenades and impressive *fin de siècle* mansions, set against a majestic backdrop of snow-clad mountains. The city is home to the largest number of museums in Switzerland, with over 50 attractions revealing every aspect of Zuricher life from toys to tourism. The Kunsthaus gallery and the traditional Schweizerisches Landesmuseum count among the nation's top museums. Most of the main sights lie in and around the charming, car-free Old Town in the city centre. The remainder are easily accessible by the super-efficient tram network. Should you get lost, there is a

The Old Town in Zurich

Zurich centre with the Grossmünster in the background

variety of unmissable landmarks to help you get your bearings, including the graceful spires of the three magnificent city-centre churches that pierce the skyline – Kirche St Peter, the Grossmünster and Fraumünster.

The most ancient quarter of the Old Town lies on the western bank of the River Limmat, and contains many restored historic mansions and guildhalls within its maze of hilly cobbled alleyways. On the eastern bank of the River Limmat, the pretty Niederdorf district forms the eastern half of the Altstadt, with its cobbled streets, romantic shuttered houses and chic art and design boutiques. This is also one of the city's main nightlife districts, brimming with bars, restaurants and cafés.

The latest addition to the city is trendy Zurich West, a former industrial neighbourhood that is quickly being reinvented, and factories, power stations and breweries are being converted into state-of-the-art museums, theatres, restaurants, bars and dance clubs. Central Zurich is the district of high finance and glamorous shops. The main artery – broad, leafy Bahnhofstrasse – counts among the world's most sophisticated shopping boulevards, and is where all Zurichers come to promenade and shop. It leads down to the city playground – Lake Zurich – popular for boating, strolling, swimming, sunbathing, barbecuing and people-watching. No trip to Zurich is complete without a mini-cruise on the lake. Choose from a variety of excursions, ranging from nostalgic paddle-steamer tours to a fondue sunset cruise.

Zurich Tourism, Hauptbahnhof.
Tel: (044) 215 40 00.
www.zuerich.com

Shopping for high-end goods in Zurich

Bahnhofstrasse

This world-famous, car-free shopping mile is the most overt manifestation of the country's wealth. With its exclusive haute couture boutiques, world-renowned jewellers, watchmakers, confectioners and celebrated banks, it epitomises the sophistication, quality and financial prowess of the city. Most major Swiss banks have their headquarters in or around its main square, Paradeplatz, and although the streets are not exactly 'paved with gold', the vaults that power Switzerland's financial centre lie immediately beneath the pavements. Bahnhofstrasse stretches from the Hauptbahnhof (Main Station) to Bürkliplatz, the main departure point for boat trips on Lake Zurich, and its bars and cafés offer some of the best people-watching in town.
Bahnhofstrasse. www.bahnhofstrasse-zuerich.ch. Tram Nos: 6, 7, 11, 13 (Bahnhofstrasse); Tram Nos: 2, 6, 7, 8, 9, 11, 13 (Paradeplatz); Tram Nos: 2, 8, 9, 11 (Bürkliplatz).

E G Bührle Collection

This private art collection is housed in an elegant 19th-century villa overlooking the lake. The main emphasis is on French Impressionists, with major canvases by such masters as Paul Cézanne, Claude Monet and Pierre Auguste Renoir but also works by Picasso.
Zollikerstrasse 172. Tel: (044) 422 00 86. www.buehrle.ch. Visits by appointment only. Admission charge.
Tram Nos: 2, 4 (Wildbachstrasse).

Kunsthalle Zurich and Migros Museum für Gegenwartskunst (Migros Museum for Contemporary Art)

For a taste of Zurich's innovative contemporary art scene, visit these two remarkable museums, housed in bright, white, lofty rooms in the former Löwenbräu brewery. The Migros Museum contains a massive permanent collection, while the Kunsthalle contains temporary

exhibitions for up-and-coming international artists.
Löwenbräuareal, Limmatstrasse 270.
Tel: (044) 272 15 15 (Kunsthalle);
(044) 277 20 50 (Migros Museum).
www.kunsthallezurich.ch;
www.migrosmuseum.ch. Open: Tue–Wed
& Fri noon–6pm; Thur noon–8pm;
Sat–Sun 11am–5pm. Admission charge.
Tram Nos: 4, 13 (Dammweg).

Kunsthaus (Museum of Fine Arts)

Switzerland's premier art gallery spans six centuries from the Middle Ages to the present, but specialises in 19th- and 20th-century Swiss art. It also contains major loans of Impressionist and Expressionist works, the largest Edvard Munch collection outside Scandinavia, and the Alberto Giacometti Foundation, which boasts the greatest collection of his sculptures in the world.
Heimplatz 1. Tel: (044) 253 84 84.
www.kunsthaus.ch. Open: Sat–Sun &

The edge of Bahnhofstrasse in Zurich

Tue 10am–6pm, Wed–Fri 10am–8pm.
Admission charge. Tram Nos: 3, 5,
8, 9 (Kunsthaus).

Schweizerisches Landesmuseum (Swiss National Museum)

This fascinating and extensive museum documents Swiss civilisation from prehistory to the present day through the world's largest collection of Swiss historical and cultural artefacts. There is a special focus on prehistory and medieval times, and an impressive collection of regional costumes, furnishings and *objets d'art* from each of the country's cantons.
Museumsstrasse 2. Tel: (044) 218 65 11.
www.musee-suisse.ch. Open: Tue–Sun
10am–5pm. Admission charge. Tram
Nos: 4, 11, 13, 14 (Bahnhofquai).

UETLIBERG (UETLI MOUNTAIN)

At 871m (2,857ft), the Uetliberg (*www.uetliberg.ch*) is affectionately known to Zurichers as the 'top of Zurich', affording sensational 360-degree vistas of the city, the lake and the Alps. It takes just 15 minutes to reach the summit by S-Bahn from the Hauptbahnhof, where a two-hour hiking route leads you along a forested mountain ridge, past lush green meadows, tinkling cowbells and chocolate-box landscapes to Felsenegg. To complete the round trip, take the cable car down to Adliswil and catch the S-Bahn back to Zurich.
S-Bahn: Uetliberg.

Walk: Zurich's Old Town

Zurich's medieval Altstadt is fascinating to explore, with its labyrinth of cobbled streets, ancient pastel-coloured houses and flower-filled squares. The west bank of the River Limmat is defined by beautiful mansions, historic guildhalls and steep cobbled lanes, while to the east, lively Niederdorf is brimming with small, quirky boutiques, bars and restaurants.

Allow 2 hours.

Start at the Rudolf-Brun-Brücke and walk along the west bank of the River Limmat through Schipfe.

1 Schipfe

One of the oldest quarters of Zurich, Schipfe is still known today for its arts, crafts and antiques shops. It contains some of the city's most attractive houses. *Climb steep Wohllebgasse then turn right up Pfalzgasse to Lindenhof.*

2 Lindenhof

This tranquil, leafy square overlooking the river is the oldest part of Zurich. *Descend Pfalzgasse and continue down Strehlgasse, across the ancient Weinplatz market square and along Storchengasse.*

3 Kirche St Peter (St Peter's Church)

Wherever you are in the Altstadt, it's hard to miss St Peter's Church, the city's oldest parish church, which has the largest clock face in Europe. *Continue to Münsterhof and the glorious Fraumünster.*

4 Fraumünster (Church of Our Lady)

The Altstadt's grandest square, Münsterhof, was once the site of a medieval pig market. Today, its crowning glory is the 13th-century Fraumünster with its elegant green spire, and five stained-glass chancel windows by Marc Chagall (1970). *Cross the river via Münsterbrücke to the Niederdorf district. Turn left along Limmat-Quai, past the riverside Rathaus (Town Hall), right up narrow Rosengasse, and right again into the pedestrianised Niederdorfstrasse.*

5 Niederdorf and Niederdorfstrasse

The Niederdorf district has a special village-like charm, with its hilly cobbled lanes, sunny courtyards, quirky boutiques and pavement cafés. *Proceed to Münstergasse.*

6 Grossmünster (Cathedral)

This impressive Romanesque and Gothic cathedral was the parish church of Huldrych Zwingli in the early 16th century and became the birthplace of the Swiss Reformation. Climb the tower for the best aerial views of the city.

Return to the river, and turn left along Uto-Quai to Bellevue.

7 Bellevue Platz

Busy Bellevue square is perhaps best known for the Sternen Grill sausage stand, and for the celebrated art nouveau Odeon Bar. Today a popular gay bar, the Odeon Bar became famous

during World War I when it was frequented by Lenin.

From here there is a wonderful lakeside walk to Zurichhorn Park.

8 Zürichhorn Park

This idyllic lakeside park is one of the most popular recreation areas for Zurichers, with its lidos, boat hire, cafés, picnic areas and ornamental gardens – there is even an outdoor cinema in summer.

Continue to the Casino and catch a boat back to the city centre.

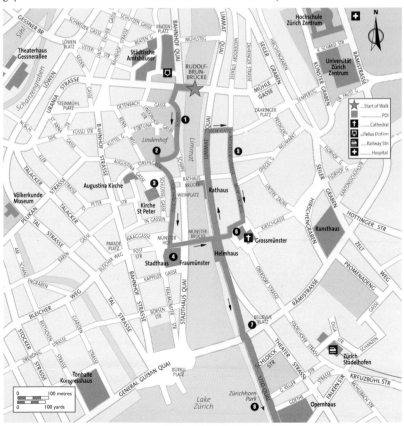

Swiss stereotypes

Think Switzerland, think clocks, chocolate, alphorns, cowbells and Heidi. Whether the Swiss like it or not, they have an undeniably stereotypical image abroad, stemming from an archetypal vision of the nation as a land of snow-capped mountains, quaint chalet villages, flower-filled meadows and yodelling cowherds. Yet some of these stereotypes are not entirely unfounded.

Alphorns

The alphorn is the very symbol of the Alps, seen all over the country on postcards and chocolate wrappers. It takes over 50 hours to carve this magnificent instrument by hand from

Cowbells and traditional costume

a sizeable block of spruce wood – some are over 3m (10ft) long. Watch them being made at Bernatone Alphornbau near Davos (*Buchlistrasse 23. Tel: (032) 633 2023. www.bernatone.ch*).

To play an alphorn requires a special breathing technique, not dissimilar to that of opera singers. Alphorns were originally used to round up the cows on the upper pastures and, although you are unlikely to hear one being played on a mountain top today, they remain an important part of Swiss heritage, and are still played recreationally in mountain bars or on the snow slopes.

Clocks

Switzerland has long been associated with clocks. However, clock manufacture started in the Black Forest, and the main pioneers were the Germans, French and English. Switzerland started producing timepieces during Calvinist times (mid-16th century), when ostentatious shows of wealth were banned, and so the jewellers of Geneva were forced to turn their attention to watchmaking, copying ideas from all the other nations. The Swiss watch

Swiss alphorns, made from spruce

industry initially thrived thanks to the country's commercial expertise and excellent banking system. Manufacture gradually spread to other areas, in particular to the Neuchâtel canton, where Abraham-Louis Perrelet devised the self winding watch and Abraham-Louis Breguet (the greatest watchmaker of all time) invented the *tourbillon* – a device that enables a watch to function irrespective of gravity. Over the centuries, Swiss watchmaking has gone from strength to strength, and today the Swiss are the undisputed masters of precision timing – and punctuality, of course!

Yodelling

Yodelling was first developed in the Swiss Alps as a method of communication, with messages yodelled from one alp to another.

It later became a vital element of traditional music in remote regions. Sadly, nowadays, most yodelling is for the benefit of tourists. Nonetheless, in cities it is becoming an increasingly popular pastime to relieve stress, and various yodelling events take place nationwide throughout the spring, culminating in July's annual Swiss Alpine Yodelling Championships, held in a different town each year.

THE SWISS FLAG

The Swiss are patriotic and thoroughly enjoy their unique 'Swissness'. Everywhere imaginable, the national flag is flown – from official buildings, mountain tops and private village gardens. It is the world's only square flag, red with a white cross. It was created originally in order to easily identify Swiss mercenaries on the battlefield. Today it has virtually become a Swiss brand – found on everything from T-shirts to beer mugs. Apparently, even the best-selling postcard in Switzerland is the Swiss flag!

Drive: Appenzellerland

It is easy to fall under the spell of Switzerland's most traditional region, with its excellent touring opportunities through picturesque villages with painted wooden houses, set in verdant hills with flower meadows and the snowy peaks of the Alpstein massif.

Allow at least one full day (longer if you wish to complete all the walks).

Start in St Gallen.

1 St Gallen

The pleasant provincial city of St Gallen has long been an important hub of the Swiss textile industry, with a tradition of lace and embroidery made by the womenfolk at home in the city and in the surrounding countryside. The intricate work from Appenzell was always particularly prized.
From St Gallen, head southwest to Herisau.

2 Herisau

This attractive town is the capital of the Protestant canton Appenzell Ausserrhoden, one of the two cantons that make up Appenzellerland (the other is Innerrhoden).
Drive via Waldstatt to Urnäsch. Then follow a winding road about 10km (6 miles) up to Schwägalp, where a cable car departs half hourly for the summit of Säntis (www.saentisbahn.ch).

3 Säntis

Snow-capped Säntis, at 2,502m (8,208ft), is the highest point of the Alpstein ridge and Appenzell's most famous peak. On a clear day, the memorable view from the top encompasses six different countries – Austria, France, Germany, Italy, Liechtenstein and Switzerland.
Return by cable car to Schwägalp. Retrace your route to Urnäsch, and follow signs eastwards towards Appenzell until the small village of Gonten.

4 Gonten

Treat yourself to a soak in the *moorbad* (peat baths) or luxuriate in mineralised water enriched with bath essences made from handpicked herbs at the Natur-Moorbad. Then set out on one of Appenzellerland's more unusual hiking trails across lush grassy meadows – where you don't need shoes – from Gonten to Appenzell.
If that sounds too energetic, drive to Appenzell instead!

5 Appenzell

The capital of the Catholic canton of Appenzell Innerrhoden is the most folkloric town of northeast Switzerland, and one of the most picturesque.

Continue through Appenzell and head south to the village of Wasserauen. From here, it is a gentle uphill walk to Seealpsee.

6 Seealpsee

This beautiful lake is the location for a popular annual folk festival that climaxes with Jodelsonntig, a yodelling of Mass on Assumption Day morning.

Retrace your steps back to Appenzell, then follow signs to Herisau. Before you reach the town, turn right to Stein.

7 Stein

The highlight of this small village is its dazzling Appenzeller Volkskunde Museum (Folklore Museum; *www.appenzeller-museum-stein.ch*). Next door, you can see how Appenzeller cheese is made at the Appenzeller Schaukäserei (*www.showcheese.ch*). *Follow signs from Stein back to St Gallen.*

Drive: Appenzellerland

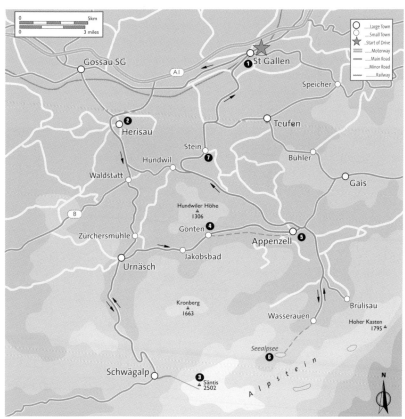

Bodensee (Lake Constance)

The popular holiday destination of Lake Constance forms a natural border between Germany, Austria and Switzerland. Visitors are drawn by its sunny, mild climate, its lovely scenery, beaches and water-sports facilities. It is possible to circumnavigate the lake by bike along a 261km (162-mile) cycle path, or alternatively you can visit the genteel towns and villages dotted along the shoreline by boat. The lake stretches 67km (41½ miles) from end to end. The largest town is Konstanz (in Germany), known for its university and impressive Münster (Cathedral).

The Swiss resorts are interspersed with vineyards and orchards, and include the old fishing hamlet of Horn; medieval Arbon with its half-timbered houses and excellent water sports; and Rorschach, with its beautiful lakeside promenade and ancient Kornhaus (granary) – a reminder of a once thriving grain trade between Switzerland and Germany. Catch a ferry from Romanshorn, the lake's largest port to Friedrichshafen (in Germany), where the Zeppelin was designed, to visit the Zeppelin Museum (*www.zeppelin-museum.de*).

Schaffhausen and Rhine Falls

Schaffhausen was once a major depot for river barges on the River Rhine. It was the only Swiss town to be bombed by allied aircraft during World War II, but thankfully its beautiful cobbled Old Town remained unharmed. Today it is considered one of Switzerland's most beautiful medieval towns. Many of the

Fireworks over Schaffhausen

houses have elaborately painted façades. The frescoes on three-storey Haus Zum Ritter in Münstergasse are considered among the most significant Renaissance frescoes north of the Alps (the originals are in the town museum).

Europe's largest and most powerful waterfalls – the mighty Rhine Falls – are situated 4km (2¹/₂ miles) downriver from Schaffhausen near Neuhausen. Impressive more for their breadth (150m/492ft) than their height (a mere 23m/75ft), they are best viewed in springtime when they are fed by the melting mountain snows. The best viewpoint is beside a turreted castle directly above the falls. Bring a raincoat! *Schaffhausen Tourismus, Herrenacker 15. Tel: (052) 632 40 20. www.schaffhauserland.ch; www.rhinefalls.com*

A hot air balloon over the Rhine Falls

St Gallen

This small, busy city contains some magnificent Art Nouveau villas (financed by a glorious textile industry) and a beautiful, traffic-free Altstadt (Old Town), but it is best known for its abbey. The roving Irish monk Gallus settled here in AD 612 and gave the city its name. The Benedictine monastery, which grew from his hermitage, became one of the most important cultural centres in the Western world until the 11th century.

The entire abbey complex, with its twin-towered baroque cathedral and former monastery complex, has been listed as a UNESCO World Heritage Site. The Stiftsbibliothek (Abbey Library; *www.stiftsbibliothek.ch*), with its priceless collection of ancient books and manuscripts, its swirling pillars, parquetry, stucco and cherubs, is one of the world's oldest libraries, and the finest example of secular rococo architecture in Switzerland.
St Gallen-Bodensee Tourismus, Bahnhofplatz 1a. Tel: (071) 227 37 37. www.st.gallen-bodensee.ch

Textilmuseum

For centuries, St Gallen has been a major hub of the Swiss textile industry, peaking in the early 20th century when embroidery was the nation's largest export industry, with St Gallen accounting for around half of the world's production. Its embroidery is still highly valued today, and this fascinating museum traces the history and stylistic developments, from linen,

lace and embroidery through to the latest fabrics used by leading haute couture houses today.
Vadianstrasse 2. Tel: (071) 222 17 44. www.textilmuseum.ch. Open: 10am–5pm. Admission charge.

Stein-am-Rhein

Stein-am-Rhein dates from 1094, and is regarded as one of the most authentic medieval towns in Switzerland. It contains the finest half-timbered houses in northeast Switzerland, with beautiful 16th-century painted façades and ornate oriel windows. Rathausplatz is arguably the most photogenic square in Switzerland. Arrive by boat from Schaffhausen (three boats a day in summer) and stay overnight to appreciate the village without the tourist hordes.
Stein-am-Rhein Tourismus, Oberstadt 3. Tel: (052) 742 20 90. www.steinamrhein.ch

Winterthur

Winterthur has more than its fair share of high-quality museums and galleries, thanks mainly to private art collector and industrialist Oskar Reinhart, who bequeathed his villa and his entire collection to the city. **Sammlung Oskar Reinhart 'Am Römerholz'** (*www. roemerholz.ch, closed until spring 2010*), in the local magnate's one-time residence, contains an assortment of acclaimed canvases from Old Masters to Impressionists, including works by Peter Paul Rubens, Hans Holbein, Pierre-

Aerial view of Stein-am-Rhein

Auguste Renoir, Pablo Picasso and others. **Museum Oskar Reinhart am Stadtgarten** (*www. museumoskarreinhart.ch*) focuses on Swiss, German and Austrian art from the 18th to the 20th centuries. The **Kunstmuseum** (Museum of Fine Arts; *www.kmw.ch, closed until spring 2010*) displays art from Claude Monet to Piet Mondrian in an impressive architectural setting, while beautiful **Villa Flora** (*www.villaflora.ch*) has a small but select group of French post-Impressionist and Fauvist works. The town's Photo Museum (*www.fotomuseum.ch*) and Swiss Photography Foundation, housed in an old warehouse, is Europe's largest photographic arts centre, with frequently changing exhibitions.
Winterthur Tourismus, Im Hauptbahnhof. Tel: (052) 267 67 00. www.winterthur-tourismus.ch

Excursion: Liechtenstein

The Principality of Liechtenstein is the world's sixth-smallest country – a narrow strip of largely mountainous land squeezed between the Rhine and the Austrian Alps, just 25km (15$\frac{1}{2}$ miles) long and 6km (3$\frac{3}{4}$ miles) wide, with a population of around 34,500. It came into existence when Viennese Prince Johann Adam von Liechtenstein bought the counties of Schellenberg (1699) and Vaduz (1712) from Germany. It later became a principality under the Holy Roman Empire and gained independence in 1866.

Today, this mini-nation is ruled by the wealthiest royal family in Europe, Prince Hans Adam II and his son, Prince Alois. It is an undeniably eccentric kingdom: the royal family live in a fairy-tale castle; their national anthem has the same tune as the British *God Save the Queen*; their language is German (although most speak an Alemannic dialect); their currency is the Swiss Franc, even though they regard themselves as entirely separate from the Swiss; and they are the world's largest exporters of false teeth. However, it is also a land of magnificent mountain scenery, lush Rhine meadows, picturesque floral Alpine villages, castles and some fantastic hiking opportunities.

The rather touristy capital, Vaduz, contains the royal castle, Schloss Vaduz, the quirky Postmuseum (Postage Stamp Museum; *Städtle 37, Vaduz. Tel: +423 239 68 46. Open: 10am–noon &* *1–5pm. Free admission*), and the Leichtensteinisches Landesmuseum (National Museum; *Städtle 43. Tel: +423 239 68 20. Open: Tue & Thur–Sun 10am–5pm, Wed 10am–8pm. Admission charge. www.landesmuseum.li*), which recounts the principality's extraordinary history. Other highlights include the popular family ski resort of Malbun, the legendary Fürstensteig trail through vertiginous landscapes, and Triesenberg's Walserhaus (*Tel: +423 262 48 59. Open: Mon–Fri 7.45–11.45am & 12.30–3.45pm, Sat 7.45–11am & 12.30–5pm. Closed: Sun. www.triesenberg.li*), documenting the Walser community, who emigrated here from Valais in the 13th century.

Liechtenstein is 1 hour by car from Zurich. Liechtenstein Tourism, Städtle 37, Vaduz. Tel: +423 239 63 00. www.tourismus.li

Schloss Vaduz, Liechtenstein

Northwest Switzerland

Northwest Switzerland is a region characterised by gentle landscapes of lush rolling valleys, waterfalls, forests, lakes and traditional villages. It also embraces part of the Röstigraben *(the invisible internal border between French- and German-speaking regions of Switzerland), which can be confusing to visitors.*

Nowhere in Switzerland is this language divide more pronounced than in Fribourg, where residents on the west bank speak French and those on the east speak German. Throughout the region, expect to see signs for Basel and for Bâle, for Murten and Morat, and for Fribourg and Freiburg. This is where two cultures merge and, as a result, the region is rich in museums, galleries and fascinating architecture.

From the stylish cities of Basel and Fribourg to the quaint chocolate-box village of Gruyères, there's something to please everyone. This is true Swiss cheese country, and most restaurants offer an astonishing array of cheese dishes as well as the ubiquitous *raclette* (s*ee p49*) and delicious regional varieties of fondue. Traditional fêtes and festivals abound, most notably in Basel with its extravagant Fasnacht parades during Lent (*see p18*) and in Fribourg at Christmas (*see p19*). It is also the cradle of Swiss watchmaking and musical box manufacture.

Sport-lovers will enjoy the Jura mountains, which form the northwestern border between Switzerland and France, just beyond Lac de Neuchâtel – the largest lake entirely in Switzerland. Somewhat off the beaten tourist track, they are a nature-lover's paradise and hugely popular for walking and cross-country skiing.

Basel
Basel, Switzerland's third-largest city, lies at the point where the French, German and Swiss borders meet, and it is surrounded by glorious countryside – the French Vosges, the German Black Forest and the Swiss Jura mountains. The city itself is bisected by the River Rhine, with **Grossbasel** (Greater Basel) on the steep left bank and **Kleinbasel** (Lesser Basel) on the right bank, but these are linked by a series of attractive bridges and four ferries powered by the strong river current (*www.faehri.ch*).

A former Roman fort in AD 374 named Basilia, and home to Switzerland's oldest university, today Basel is a major river port and an international centre of banking and the pharmaceutical industry. Its main sights include the beautifully preserved Old Town; the impressive sandstone **Münster** (Cathedral); and the striking red Renaissance **Rathaus** (Town Hall), which dominates **Marktplatz**, a colourful square and scene of a daily fruit and vegetable market. In summer months, you can join locals swimming in the River Rhine or hop aboard a river cruise (*Basler Personenschifffahrt. www.bpg.ch*) to see the sights. The city is also celebrated for its exuberant

Fasnacht (Carnival) during Lent, and its large and traditional Christmas market, but perhaps it is best known as one of the nation's leading cultural centres, boasting over 30 top-notch museums and galleries.
Basel Tourismus, Stadtcasino, Barfüsserplatz. Tel: (061) 268 68 68. www.baseltourismus.ch. Open: Mon–Fri 8.30am–6.30pm, Sat 9am–5pm, Sun & holidays 10am–4pm.

Basler Papiermühle (Basel Paper Mill)
This characterful medieval watermill contains the Swiss Museum of Paper, Writing and Printing. You can watch craftspeople at work, and make – and even print on – your own paper.

Northwest Switzerland

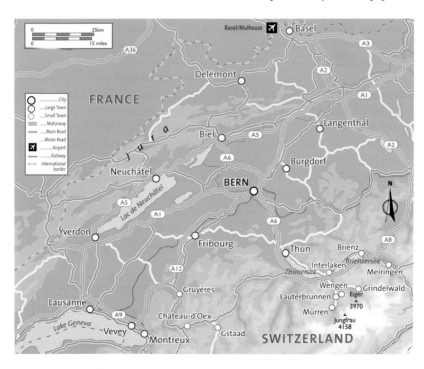

St Alban-Tal 37. Tel: (061) 225 90 90. www.papiermuseum.ch. Open: Tue–Sun 2–5pm. Admission charge. Tram No: 2 (Kunstmuseum).

Fondation Beyeler

Basel's most prestigious gallery contains a small but stunning collection of art by such greats as Paul Cézanne, Claude Monet, Henri Rousseau, Ray Lichtenstein, Alberto Giacometti, Paul Klee, Vincent van Gogh and Andy Warhol. Even the light-infused, open-plan building, designed by Italian architect Renzo Piano, is a work of art, with its floor-to-ceiling windows leading to the beautiful gardens outside.
Baselstrasse 101. Tel: (061) 645 97 00. www.beyeler.com. Open: Thur–Tue 10am–6pm, Wed 10am–8pm. Admission charge. Tram No: 6 (Fondation Beyeler).

Kunstmuseum (Fine Arts Museum)

This world-famous museum focuses on two main periods. The highlight of the vast medieval collection is the world's largest number of works by the prolific Holbein family. The smaller collection contains impressive 19th- and 20th-century canvases by Pablo Picasso, Salvador Dalí, Paul Klee, Edvard Munch, Georges Braque and the Impressionists.
St Alban-Graben 16. Tel: (061) 206 62 62. www.kunstmuseumbasel.ch. Open: Tue–Sun 10am–5pm. Admission charge. Tram Nos: 2, 15 (Kunstmuseum).

Museum Jean Tinguely

Designed by the celebrated Swiss architect, Mario Botta, this striking museum provides a fitting backdrop for the witty, mechanical sculptures of Switzerland's best-loved artist, Jean Tinguely. His 'kinetic' creations resemble those of a mad scientist, made out of scrap metal, springs, wheels, feathers and bits of everyday junk. There is also an impressive Tinguely Fountain outside the Kunsthalle in the city centre.
Paul Sacher-Anlage 2. Tel: (061) 681 93 20. www.tinguely.ch. Open: Tue–Sun 11am–7pm. Admission charge. Bus Nos: 31, 36 (Tinguely-Museum).

Fribourg

This picturesque medieval city on the River Sarine is the capital of the Fribourg canton. Despite its carefully preserved medieval centre, it is a cosmopolitan, forward-looking city that takes pride in the region's contemporary arts as well as its local traditions and festivals. One of the most unusual features of Fribourg is the funicular (cable railway) that links the upper part of the city to the lower reaches. It is the last of its kind in Europe to run solely on water and offers spectacular city vistas.

Explore the **Old Town** by mini-train (*May–Sept Tue–Sun; Oct weekends only*), with its atmospheric alleyways and cobbled streets adorned with churches, countless listed medieval houses, elegant Renaissance fountains and the Bern Bridge – an ancient covered bridge made of wood. The Gothic **Cathédrale St-Nicolas** (Cathedral of St Nicholas) is the focal point of the Old Town with its magnificent Art Nouveau stained-glass windows and impressive organ, once played by composer Franz Liszt. Climb the tower for a memorable bird's-eye view.

Fribourg's museums range from the traditional, including the Musée d'Art et d'Histoire (Museum of Art and History; *www.fr.ch/mahf*) and the Musée d'Histoire Naturelle (Museum of Natural History; *www.fr.ch/mhn*) with its botanical gardens, to the small and quirky: beer, puppet, sewing machine and miniature railway museums. The **Espace Jean Tinguely & Niki de Saint Phalle** (*www.fr.ch/mahf. Closed. Mon & Tue. Admission charge*), housed in a former tram depot, is dedicated to the city's two best-known artists. Their light-hearted sculptures are also dotted around the city as part of a 'Sculpture Trail' of 40 installations by well-known Swiss and international artists *(Rue de Morat 2. Tel: (026) 305 51 70). Fribourg Tourisme, avenue de la Gare 1. Tel: (026) 350 11 11. www.fribourgtourisme.ch*

Gruyères

This idyllic, medieval, walled village is a veritable tourist honeypot, best known for its cheese, fairy-tale castle and surrounding countryside of verdant pre-Alpine pastures. The handsome village is car-free between Easter and October (and on Sundays year round) and has just one street.
La Gruyère Tourism. Tel: (026) 919 85 00. www.la-gruyere.ch

Château de Gruyères (Gruyères Castle)

A massive gate leads from the main street to the imposing castle, which reflects the rich history of the Counts of Gruyères over eight centuries. Highlights include Flemish tapestries, heraldic stained glass, often featuring a crane (*grue* in French) that was part of the Counts' crest, and some noteworthy murals by Camille Corot, who lived here for a while.
Tel: (026) 921 21 02. www.chateau-gruyeres.ch. Open: Apr–Oct 9am–6pm; Nov–Mar 10am–4.30pm. Admission charge.

Fromagerie d'Alpage (Mountain Cheese Dairy)

Follow the two-hour Cheese Dairy Path from Gruyères, through rich pastures of

Neuchâtel castle

bell-ringing cattle, up to a cosy 17th-century chalet to see how cheese is made in the traditional way – in a huge cauldron over a fireplace.
Moléson. Tel: (026) 921 10 44. www.fromagerie-alpage.ch. Open: May–Sept 9.30am–7pm. Cheese-making demonstrations: June–Aug, Oct–Apr & May Sat & Sun 10am–2.30pm; Sept daily 10am. Admission charge.

Maison du Fromage (House of Cheese)

The train touristique de Gruyères (touristic train) runs between the castle and the Maison du Fromage at the entrance to the village, which offers demonstrations of cheese-making.
Tel: (026) 921 84 00. www.lamaisondugruyere.ch. Open: June–Sept 9am–7pm; Oct–May 9am–6pm. Cheese-making demonstrations: 9–11am & 12.30–2.30pm. Admission charge.

Jura

The Jura is one of Switzerland's best-kept secrets and the centre of the Swiss watchmaking industry. The most recent of the nation's 26 cantons, created in 1979, it comprises the Jura plateau with the Jura mountains beyond, which stretch southwest to the Canton of Vaud. The term 'Jurassic' derives from these mountains, which date from that era. In contrast to the Alps, they are low, forested and gently undulating, and especially popular for mountain biking and hiking.

In winter, the Jura is one of Europe's largest cross-country ski areas. In summer, it is a walkers' paradise, with such natural sites of breathtaking beauty as the 27m (88ft) high Saut du Doubs waterfall; the tranquil Lac des Taillières (Lake Taillières) at La Brevine; the Étang de Gruère (Gruère Pond) at the Centre Nature Les Cerlatez (nature reserve); the Gorge de l'Areuse at Boudry; and the dramatic Creux-du-Van, a gigantic limestone cirque 1km ($2/3$ mile) in diameter, near Noraigue.

The region is also known for its arts and crafts, especially its timepieces and musical boxes. Visit the Musée International d'Horlogerie at La Chaux-de-Fonds (*Rue des Musées 29. Tel: (032) 967 68 61. www.mih.ch. Open: Tue–Sun 10am–5pm. Admission charge*) to discover how the town came to be the epicentre of the Swiss watchmaking industry in the late 18th and 19th centuries. Sainte-Croix and L'Auberson in the Jura Vaudois have over 200 years of musical box manufacture, as illustrated at the enchanting Musée Baud (*Grand-Rue 23, L'Auberson. Tel: (024) 454 24 84. www.museebaud.ch. Open: July–Sept 2–5pm; Oct–June Sat 2–5pm, Sun 10am–noon & 2–6pm. Admission charge*).
www.juratourisme.ch

Neuchâtel

The small, gracious university town of Neuchâtel lies on the northwestern shore of Lac de Neuchâtel, and is the capital of the canton of the same name.

Its inhabitants are reputed to speak the purest French in Switzerland. The car-free Old Town centre is best explored by tourist train or on foot, with the help of eight *promenades touristiques* (tourist trails) marked around the town and along its lengthy, lakeside promenade. The medieval core of the town was once described by Alexandre Dumas as 'a toytown carved out of butter', due to the yellow hue of the ancient limestone houses that line the fountain-splashed squares.

The town is dominated by the Renaissance castle (*Open: Apr–Sept, 45-min guided tours only, Tue–Fri 10am, 11am, noon, 2pm, 3pm, 4pm, Sat–Mon 2pm, 3pm, 4pm*), the mainly Gothic **Église Collégiale** (University Church) and the medieval **Prison Tower** (*Open: Apr–Sept*), which afford sweeping views of the lake and the surrounding countryside. Neuchâtel is situated at the foot of the Jura mountains and surrounded by vineyards. The **Fête des Vendanges** (Harvest Festival) on the last weekend in September is one of the town's annual highlights.

Tourisme Neuchâtelois, Hôtel des Postes. Tel: (032) 889 68 90.
www.neuchateltourisme.ch

Musée d'Art et d'Histoire (Museum of Art and History)

Discover some local history and admire three astonishing 18th-century clockwork automata by local watchmaker, Pierre Jaquet-Droz. Considered by some to be the oldest examples of the computer, they are set in motion on the first Sunday of each month (*at 2pm, 3pm & 4pm*).
Esplanade Léopold-Robert 1. Tel: (032) 717 79 25. www.mahn.ch. Open: Tue–Sun 11am–6pm.
Admission charge.

Thousands flock to Gruyères for its beauty, and its cheese

Cheese

Think Switzerland, think cheese! *Käse, chäs, chääs, fromage, formaggio* – call it what you will, but there's no denying that Swiss cheese is a staple of Swiss cuisine and a national pastime. The individual varieties are savoured by the Swiss like wines in France or whiskies in Scotland. In fact, they take it all so seriously, that they even have websites devoted to the most popular varieties (*see box*).

Cheeses great and small

The most typical image of Swiss cheese is Emmentaler (*www.emmentaler.ch*). This delicious, smooth, holey cheese from the Emme valley, east of Bern, is a veritable Swiss icon and one of the nation's oldest varieties. It is also among the most difficult to produce due to its complicated fermentation process, which requires the blending of three different types of bacteria to create its distinctive flavour. One of these bacteria (*Propionibacter shermani*) produces bubbles of carbon dioxide when added to the cheese mixture. These bubbles go on to become the cheese's distinctive holes, or 'eyes'.

The other big cheese is Gruyère (*www.gruyere.com*) – the favourite cheese of the Swiss – a rich, sweet, slightly nutty-flavoured hard cheese with a stronger flavour than Emmentaler. Visit the factory at Gruyères (*see p47*) to see it being made into massive rounds, each weighing around 45kg (100lb).

Although most Swiss cheese is produced in the valleys, the tradition of individual *Alpkäse* (Alpine cheese,

Raclette cheese from Valais

Stored cheese in Gruyères

'La Gruyère', from Bulle to Montbovon in the canton of Fribourg. After cocktails in the saloon-wagon, try your hand at making your own traditional cheese fondue, followed by meringues with double cream for dessert – another scrumptious local speciality (*Retro Train. Tel: (026) 913 05 12. www.tpf.ch.*
Excursions: Nov–mid-Apr Fri–Sun, 4 hours' duration.
Reservations essential).

The other top Swiss cheese dish is the Valaisan *raclette* (from the French verb *racler*, to scrape), with slabs of tangy Raclette cheese (*www.raclette-suisse.ch*) traditionally melted over a wood fire (or in a special machine at your table), then scraped on top of new potatoes, tiny pickled onions and gherkins.

also called *Bergkäse, fromage des alpes* and *formaggio alpe*) still lives on in the high pastures during summer months – small, rich and characterful cheeses are handmade from raw, unprocessed cows' and goats' milk. Try them in specialist cheese shops and markets around the country.

Top dishes

Gruyère is one of the main ingredients in a cheese fondue (from the French verb *fondre*, to melt). The most common fondue is served *moitié-moitié* (50 per cent Gruyère, 50 per cent Vacherin Fribourgeois) with cubes of crusty bread. Regional variations include *fondue Fribourgeoise* (just Vacherin), *fondue Neuchâteloise* (Gruyère and Emmentaler) and *fondue Vaudoise* (just Gruyère).

Fondue fans will enjoy a fun evening out aboard the Retro Train

REGIONAL CHEESES

Top regional cheeses include Appenzeller cheese, reputedly one of the smelliest cheeses in the world (*www.appenzeller.ch*), used in such delicious dishes as *Chäshöornli* (cheese and potato mini-dumplings) and *Chäsflade* (cheese tart with coriander); Sbrinz, the Swiss equivalent of parmesan, originating from Brienz (*www.sbrinz.ch*); spicy Tête de Moine, first made at Bellelay monastery in the Jura, hence the name 'Monk's Head' (*www.tetedemoine.ch*); creamy, semi-hard Tilsiter from the Bodensee region (*www.tilsiter.ch*); and herby Schabziger, from Glarus, with its distinctive green conical form (*www.schabziger.ch*).

Bernese Oberland

The German-speaking Bernese Oberland (Bernese Highland) lies at the heart of Switzerland, and contains some of the nation's most spectacular scenery, including the Alpine giants, the Eiger (ogre), Mönch (monk) and Jungfrau (virgin). The Jungfraujoch, the highest railway station in Europe at 3,454m (11,331ft), counts among the country's top tourist attractions, with its unsurpassable 360-degree Alpine vistas. The Jungfrau region is also the birthplace of modern-day tourism.

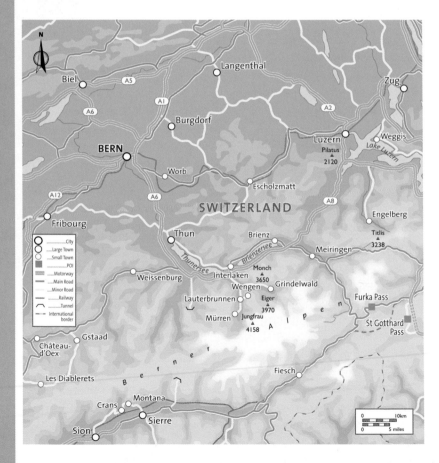

Jungfraujoch – the 'Top of Europe'

The Bernese Oberland is a popular all-year playground, thanks to its majestic snow-covered landscapes, icy glacier gorges, dramatic waterfalls, mild lakeside promenades, and a comprehensive network of paddle steamers, cable cars and cogwheel railways accessing hundreds of kilometres of walking trails through floral Alpine pastures. In recent years, it has also become a top destination for adventure sports. Switzerland is now one of the world's largest adventure sports destinations, and the gracious lakeside resort of Interlaken is its hub.

The region also embraces the crystal-clear lakes of the Thunersee and Brienzersee, numerous ski hot spots (including Gstaad, Wengen, Mürren and Grindelwald) and the beautiful city of Bern. Small, sleepy and picturesque, with its medieval, arcaded Altstadt (Old Town), it is easy to forget that this is the capital of Switzerland and home of the Swiss parliament. The canton of Bern, which encompasses most of the Bernese Oberland, is the second largest in Switzerland.

Bern

Bern (Berne in French) has been the federal capital of Switzerland since 1848. As capital cities go, it must be one of the most picturesque and atmospheric. Located on the River Aare and surrounded by steep, wooded hills, it feels more like a village than a capital, with its pedestrian cobbled streets, beautiful medieval Altstadt (Old Town) and tiny population of less than 130,000.

Bern was founded in 1191, on a peninsula in the River Aare, which afforded natural protection on three sides. In the late Middle Ages, it was the largest and most powerful city-state north of the Alps. In 1405, most of the city was burned to the ground, but it was rebuilt almost immediately. The resulting cluster of cobbled lanes, with their ornate sandstone arcaded buildings and countless wells and fountains, has remained intact for centuries and, in 1983, was listed as a UNESCO World Heritage Site. The city centre is easy to explore on foot, with the major landmarks of the river, the Käfigturm (Prison Tower), the lacy cathedral spire, and the celebrated Zytglogge (Clock Tower) to help you get your bearings.

The centre of city life is the longest covered shopping promenade in Europe – 6km (3³/₄ miles) of arcades adjoining flower- and flag-bedecked medieval houses, and containing hundreds of small boutiques, cafés and restaurants, many within atmospheric vaulted cellars. There is also a traditional weekly market on Tuesday and Saturday mornings, and a celebrated traditional Onion Market each November (see p19).

Bern Tourismus, Hauptbahnhof. Tel: (031) 328 12 12. www.Berninfo.com.

Bern, surrounded by hills and mountains

Christmas lights in Bern Altstadt

June–Sept daily 9am–8.30pm; Oct–May Mon–Sat 9am–6.30pm, Sun 10am–5pm.

Kunstmuseum (Museum of Fine Arts)
One of Switzerland's top galleries, with over 3,000 paintings and sculptures from all eras but focusing mainly on Swiss and international artworks from the 19th and early 20th centuries.
Hodlerstrasse 8–12. Tel: (031) 328 09 44. www.kunstmuseumbern.ch. Open: Tue 10am–9pm, Wed–Sun 10am–5pm. Admission charge. Bus Nos: 20, 21, 11 (Bollwerk).

Münster (Cathedral)
Bern's cathedral is a magnificent late-Gothic basilica with a triple nave and the highest spire in Switzerland. As you enter the impressive, lofty interior, look out for a beautiful depiction of the Last Judgement, with more than 200 figures carved above the main portal. Just inside the door, climb the narrow spiral staircase up the tower for a memorable aerial vista of the city and the Alps beyond.
*Münsterplatz 1. Tel: (031) 312 04 62. www.bernermuenster.ch.
Open: Mon–Fri 10am–noon & 2–4pm, Sat 10am–noon & 2–5pm, Sun 11.30am– 4pm (winter); Mon–Sat 10am–5pm, Sun 11.30am–5pm (summer) (last admission to tower 30min before closing).
Bus Nos: 12, 30 (Rathaus).*

Zentrum Paul Klee
This extraordinary wave-shaped museum on the outskirts of Bern contains the world's largest collection of works by Paul Klee, Bern's most famous artist, including 4,000 works donated by private collectors, Maurice and Martha Müller. Elegant and futuristic, the gallery was designed by Renzo Piano (designer of the Pompidou Centre in Paris) and inaugurated in 2005. There is a children's museum in the basement that stages regular art workshops.
*Monument im Fruchtland 3.
Tel: (031) 359 01 01.
www.zpk.org.
Open: Tue–Sun 10am–5pm.
Admission charge.
Bus No: 12 (Zentrum Paul Klee).*

Walk: Bern's Old Town

Wind back the clocks and explore Bern's charming Altstadt (Old Town) – one of Europe's best-preserved medieval towns with its sandstone houses and fountain-splashed squares, where the cityscape has barely changed for centuries.

Start in Bahnhofplatz, beside the early 18th-century Heiliggeistkirche (Church of the Holy Ghost), and head eastwards up Spittalgasse. Allow 2 hours.

1 Pfeiferbrunnen and Bärenplatz

The colourful Pfeiferbrunnen (Piper Fountain), with its bagpiper sculpture, is one of a dozen fascinating medieval fountains in the Old Town. Further up Spittalgasse, Bärenplatz is dominated by the huge 13th-century Käfigturm (Prison Tower).

Pass under the tower into the Altstadt's main shopping street, Marktgasse, and past the Musketeer Fountain to Kornhausplatz.

2 Kornhausplatz

The impressive Kornhaus was once an 18th-century granary. Now it has been converted into a popular restaurant (*see p159*). Here too, on the left, is the ancient Kindlifresserbrunnen (Child-eating Ogre Fountain), based on a local Carnival figure, and Bern's celebrated Zytgloggeturm (Clock Tower), which acted as the town's west gate during the 12th century. Its astronomical calendar clock dates back to 1530 and its clockwork figurines

perform three minutes before the hour.
Continue eastwards along Kramgasse.

3 Kramgasse

Kramgasse is one of the prettiest streets in the Old Town, and several of its attractive houses are decorated with turrets, spires and oriel windows. The Zähringer Fountain here is devoted to the city founder, Duke Berchtold von Zähringen, and shows the city's emblem, the Bern bear, together with the Zähringer coat of arms.
Continue along Kramgasse.

4 Haus Einstein (Einstein House)

On the right at Kramgasse No 49 is the former home of scientist Albert Einstein, who developed his special theory of relativity here in 1905. His apartment has remained essentially unchanged for over 100 years. Just past Einstein House, beside the Konservatorium für Musik (Music Conservatory), the impressive Samson

Fountain symbolises strength.
*Continue eastwards into
Gerechtigkeitsgasse with its famous
Justice Fountain, depicting Justice
with worshipping subjects at
her feet. Cross the river at the end
of the street.*

5 Bärengraben

The Bärengraben (Bear Pits) are
Bern's most visited sight, and home
to three Pyrenean brown bears.
According to legend, the first animal
to be killed by the city's founder,
Duke Berchtold von Zähringen,
while hunting was a bear, giving the
city its name. The Bernshow here
provides a short 3-D multimedia
overview of the city's history, with
viewings every 20 minutes.
*Return across Nydeggbrücke, turn left
into Junkerngasse and continue on
to Münsterplatz.*

6 Münster (Cathedral)

The late-Gothic Cathedral of St Vincent
is Switzerland's largest sacred building
(*see p53*). Climb the tower for dazzling
views of the historic city centre against
a majestic Alpine backdrop. Cobbled
Münsterplatz, with its Moses Fountain,
is the venue for the popular annual
Christmas market.
*Head westwards along Münstergasse and
into Amthausgasse until you reach
Bundesplatz (Federal Square).*

7 Bundeshaus (Federal Parliament)

The Swiss government resides at the
impressive Bundeshaus, which was built
in 1902 in Italian Renaissance style.
The fountain in the square has 26
jets, each representing a canton.
In summer months, they gush upwards
every half-hour, much to the delight
of passers-by.

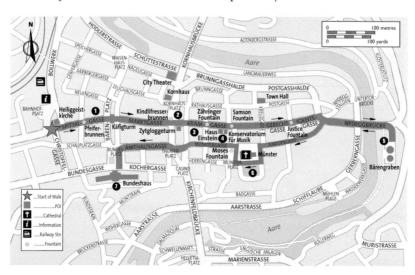

Modern architecture

There's more to Swiss architecture than picture-perfect wooden Alpine chalets festooned with geraniums. Switzerland has always been innovative in design and currently has some of the leading architects of the world.

Herzog and de Meuron

Basel may seem an unlikely venue for contemporary architecture. However, it is the home of Jacques Herzog and Pierre de Meuron – two internationally renowned architects,

Modernity in the mountains – the Hotel Tschuggen in Arosa

best known for the Tate Modern in London, the CaixaForum Madrid and Beijing's 2008 Olympic Stadium. Herzog and de Meuron's creations in Basel include the unusual Schaulager (a spartan, polygonal gallery-cum-warehouse) and the St Jakob Park football stadium, venue of Euro 2008's opening match.

Herzog and de Meuron have competition on their home soil: Italian architect Renzo Piano's Beyeler Foundation (*see p44*) is a striking new gallery with vast, open-plan light-infused display areas; and Mario Botta's Museum Jean Tinguely (*see p44*), with its simple brick façade, clean lines and clever use of light, is the perfect backdrop to Swiss sculptor Tinguely's madcap creations.

Mario Botta

Ticino-born Mario Botta is Switzerland's most famous living architect. His home town of Lugano is a virtual Botta showcase, full of houses, banks and office buildings showing his penchant for simple geometric forms, skylights and small, binocular-style windows. Botta's most inspired creations include the Tschuggen Bergoase Spa in Arosa, and

The KKL in Luzern

two churches in Ticino – futuristic
Santa Maria degli Angeli at Monte
Tamaro and cylindrical Chiesa di San
Giovanni Battista in Mogno (see p117).
During his formative years, Botta was
an apprentice to Le Corbusier.

Le Corbusier
Le Corbusier, born in the Jura in
1887, was arguably the most
influential and admired architect of
the 20th century, with his innovative,
modernist designs. His radical ideas
were given full expression in his 1923
book *Vers une architecture* (*Towards a
New Architecture*), which is still the
best-selling architecture book of all
time, and contains his maxim 'The
house is a machine for living in'.
He designed the Heidi-Weber-Haus
in Zurich as the culmination of his
studies and to serve as a museum of
his life and works. A bold, minimalist

steel-and-glass building with brightly
coloured enamel blocks, it was his last
building – completed posthumously in
1967 (he died in 1965) on the shores
of the Zurichsee.

It seems fitting that Le Corbusier's
legacy of 20th-century innovation
found its final expression in Zurich, as
the city has been a centre of artistic
and liberal thought for centuries.
Today, its converted industrial spaces
of Züri-West, including the celebrated
Schiffbau (see p157), lead the way
in urban regeneration as supreme
examples of post-modern
21st-century industrial architecture.

Twenty-first century design
Across the country, modernist
buildings are redefining formerly
traditional cities. Luzern has the KKL
(Kultur und Kongresszentrum Luzern,
see p92) by French architect Jean
Nouvel – an international masterpiece
of modern architecture with a striking
roof that juts out over the lake. Bern
has Renzo Piano's futuristic, wave-like
new Zentrum Paul Klee (see p53), and
St Gallen has the 'Mussel', designed
by Spanish architect, Santiago
Calatrava – an extraordinary mussel-
shaped police control room with a
moveable roof. Thanks to these
strident buildings, Switzerland looks
set to remain at the cutting edge of
post-modern architecture.

The skiing village of Grindelwald

Grindelwald

Picturesque Grindelwald (1,034m/ 3,392ft above sea level) is at the heart of a sensational skiing region, embracing Interlaken, Wengen and Mürren, and surrounded by impressive 4,000m (13,125ft) peaks, including the celebrated Eiger, Mönch and Jungfrau. It is a popular year-round resort for adventure sports, including mountaineering, ice climbing, canyon jumping and paragliding. It also has the world's longest toboggan course and the longest aerial gondola ride to Männlichen.

Grindelwald Tourismus. Tel: (033) 854 12 12. www.grindelwald.com

Gstaad

Surprisingly, the glittering ski resort of Gstaad, twinned with Cannes, and attracting such celebrities as Sean Connery, Paris Hilton, Roger Moore and a host of minor royals, is a tiny one-street village, better known for its designer shopping and palatial hotels than its skiing. Scene of the celebrated Swiss Open tennis tournament and the Yehudi Menuhin Music Festival in summer, it is also popular for hiking in the surrounding Saarnenland.

Office du tourisme, Promenade.
Tel: (033) 748 81 81. www.gstaad.ch

Interlaken

This sedate lakeside town is the tourist capital of the Bernese Oberland. Idyllically located between the lakes of Thun and Brienz, and encircled by mountains, Interlaken enjoys a mild, stable climate and has been a popular summer resort for over 300 years. Nowadays, it is one of Switzerland's top adventure sports destinations, known for its river-rafting, canyoning, bungee jumping, skydiving, snowshoe trekking, horse riding, waterskiing and windsurfing. In winter, it offers easy access to the massive Jungfrau ski region.

In the town centre, the Höhe-Mätte park contains the remains of a 12th-century Augustinian monastery, and the attractive lakeside promenade is fringed with hotels, cafés and gardens. Climb aboard a paddle steamer to visit the pretty villages surrounding the lakes.

Interlaken Tourism, Höheweg 37. Tel: (033) 826 53 00. www.interlaken.ch

Touristik-Museum der Jungfrau-Region (Regional Museum of Tourism)

Tourism first began in Interlaken in 1690 when Margrave Frederic Albert of Brandenberg travelled to the Jungfrau massif. He was followed by such luminaries as Johann Wolfgang von Goethe, Felix Mendelssohn, Mark Twain, Richard Wagner and the first package tourists in the early 19th century. This, Switzerland's first regional tourism museum, in the old district of Unterseen across the River Aare, documents the development of travel and tourism here. The nearby parish church is one of the region's most photographed sights, with its late-Gothic tower flanked by the peaks of the Mönch and the Jungfrau.

Stadthausplatz, Obere Gasse 28. Tel: 033 822 98 39. www.unterseen.ch/museum. Open: May–mid-Oct Tue–Sun 2–5pm. Admission charge.

Mürren and Wengen

The traffic-free villages of Mürren and Wengen lie on sunny terraces high above the glacial Lauterbrunnen Valley. Wengen (1,274m/4,179ft above sea level) is an excellent family resort, easily reached by cogwheel railway from Lauterbrunnen, with superb skiing and hiking in the Männlichen-Kleine Scheidegg and Eiger glacier areas.

At 1,650m (5,413ft) above sea level, charming picture-postcard Mürren is the highest-altitude ski resort in the Bernese Oberland, reached by cable car from Stechelberg. Popular mountain-top excursions include Allmendhubel for summer hiking and winter skiing and sledding, and the Piz Gloria solar-powered revolving restaurant atop the Schilthorn (2,970m/9,743ft) – the dramatic location for the James Bond movie *On Her Majesty's Secret Service*. Clips of the film can be viewed at the Touristorama at the summit.

Wengen Tourismus. Tel: (033) 855 14 14. Mürren Tourismus. Tel: (033) 856 86 86. www.wengen-muerren.ch

Gstaad at twilight

Excursion: Jungfraujoch Rail

At 3,454m (11,331ft), the Jungfraujoch is the highest-altitude railway station in Europe and affords some of Switzerland's most spectacular Alpine views. It is situated at the heart of the UNESCO World Heritage listed Jungfrau-Aletsch-Bietschhorn region – the most glaciated part of the Alps.

Take the Wengernalp cogwheel railway (WAB) from Interlaken Ost to Lauterbrunnen. Allow a full day.

Lauterbrunnen

This small resort is situated in a beautiful glaciated valley in the Alps, with 72 waterfalls and nearly 400 mountain streams.
The next train climbs past Wengen and circles around the peak of the Lauberhorn.

Lauberhorn

This mountain (2,470m/8,103ft) marks the start point of the Lauberhornrennen (Lauberhorn Ski Race). Inaugurated in 1930, and at over 4km (2½ miles), it is the longest, oldest downhill ski race in the annual World Cup calendar.
Continue on the train up to Kleine Scheidegg (2,061m/6,761ft).

Kleine Scheidegg

The railway station here is situated at the foot of the notorious Eiger Nordwand (North Face), one of the world's most challenging mountaineering ascents.

Straightforward walking trails descend to Grindelwald (allow 4 hours) and Wengen (allow 2 hours), or there is a more advanced hike up to the Eigergletscher train station. From here, the Jungfrau railway begins its remarkable journey up to the eternal glacier world of the 'Top of Europe'.
The first stop after Kleine Scheidegg is at the Eigergletscher station (2,320m/7,611ft).

Eigergletscher

The awesome Eiger glacier is best viewed from the ridge behind the station. There is also a clearly signed 'Eiger Trail' across scree slopes directly beneath the Eiger, with some of the best views of the sheer north face after about half an hour's hike. The Eigergletscher is also known for its panoramic restaurant and its polar dog kennels. There has been a dog colony here for nearly 100 years. The dogs were originally used to transport provisions and mail during the

construction of the railway. Today they provide sledge rides for visitors at the Jungfraujoch.
Continue on the Jungfrau railway through the tunnel behind the notorious Eiger Nordwand (North Face).

Eigerwand and Eismeer

The train stops for five minutes at two spectacular viewing stations with massive observation windows cut from the rock, overlooking the stark and dramatic white landscapes of the Eiger (3,970m/13,024ft) and Mönch (4,099m/13,448ft).
Continue to the underground railway station at the summit.

Jungfraujoch – the 'Top of Europe'

Snow is guaranteed 365 days a year on the Jungfrau plateau beneath the mighty peak of the Jungfrau

(4,158m/13,641ft), and, on a clear day, the breathtaking views extend as far as the Vosges mountains in France and the Black Forest in Germany. The mountain takes its name (Virgin) from the white-clad Augustinian nuns of medieval Interlaken.

The Jungfraujoch also marks the start of the Great Aletsch glacier (*see p82*). At a staggering 23.6km (14^{1}/$_{2}$ miles), it is the longest glacier in the Alps. An Ice Gateway links the plateau with the Ice Palace, with its amazing ice sculptures. Further attractions include: a High-Alpine Research Exhibition, a glacier trek, a ski and snowboard park, dog-sled rides in summer, and the 'Top of Europe' restaurant.
Jungfraubahnen, Höheweg 37, Interlaken. Tel: (033) 828 72 33. www.jungfraubahn.ch Return to Interlaken by train via Grindelwald.

The Jungfrau railway, beneath its ultimate destination

Drive: Thun to the Gotthard Tunnel

The lakes of Thunersee and Brienzersee form a gateway from northern Switzerland to the high Alps of the south, and offer an endlessly changing landscape, from flower-filled meadows, tumbling waterfalls and glassy lakes to the impressive glaciers and snow-clad peaks of Switzerland's celebrated passes. Allow two days.

Start your journey at Thun.

1 Thun

The delightful town of Thun, with its medieval hilltop castle and cobbled Old Town, straddles the River Aare at the northernmost tip of Thunersee, a lovely lake bordered by mountains.

Drive along the photogenic northern shoreline, past the funicular at Beatenbucht to St-Beatus-Höhlen.

2 St-Beatus-Höhlen (St Beatus Caves)

This maze of caves and underground lakes apparently sheltered St Beatus, who brought Christianity to Switzerland in the 6th century. Today, the caves are famed for their spectacular chambers of stalactites and stalagmites (*Tel: (033) 841 16 43. www.beatushoehlen.ch. Open: Apr–mid-Oct. Caves: only guided tours every 30 min 10.30am–5pm. Museum: 11.30am–5.30pm).*

Continue to Interlaken (see p58), then follow the RN6/11 along the northern shore of Brienzersee.

3 Brienz and Brienzersee (Lake Brienz)

Lake Brienz is reputedly the cleanest lake in Switzerland, surrounded by forested slopes and pretty villages. One of the best lake views is from the Brienzer Rothorn (2,350m/7,709ft), accessed by a nostalgic steam-cogwheel railway from the main town of Brienz (*Tel: (033) 952 22 22. www.brienz-rothorn-bahn.ch*).

Follow signs to the Freilichtmuseum Ballenberg, 3km (1¾ miles) east of Brienz.

4 Freilichtmuseum Ballenberg (Open-Air Museum Ballenberg)

Over 100 ancient buildings from all over Switzerland have been carefully preserved here to illustrate the varied architecture of each region. Combined with demonstrations of typical crafts, the museum creates a vivid impression of rural life in past times.

Tel: (033) 952 10 30. www.ballenberg.ch. Open: mid-Apr–Oct 10am–5pm.

Return to Brienz and head southwards on the RN6/11 to Meiringen.

5 Meiringen

This old town has two claims to fame: it is said that sweet meringues were first created here when Napoleon came to town – a fact supported by all the local patisseries; and the nearby Reichenbach Falls is where Arthur Conan Doyle's fictional detective Sherlock Holmes fell to his death. The small Sherlock Holmes Museum contains a complete replica of his study in Baker Street, London (*Tel: (033) 971 41 41. www.sherlockholmes.ch. Open: May–Sept Tue–Sun 1.30–6pm; Oct–Apr Wed & Sun 4.30–6pm*). Just south of Meiringen, an old funicular carries visitors to a viewing platform above the thundering, 120m (393ft) high waterfall (*Tel: (033) 972 90 10. www. reichenbachfall.ch. Open: daily May–June & Sept–Oct 9–11.45am & 1–5.45pm; July–Aug 9am–6pm*). *Continue southwards to Innertkirchen, then wind along the RN6 over the majestic Grimsel Pass (open only in*

summer) with its stupendous views of snowy peaks, lakes and glaciers. Join the RN19 at Gletsch and head eastwards to the Furka Pass.

6 Furka Pass

One of the most scenic passes in Switzerland, this 32km (20-mile) mountain pass is open only in summer and takes about two-and-a-half hours to drive, with views of the Rhône glacier, and the Bernese and Valais Alps. *Proceed eastwards to Andermatt.*

7 Andermatt

This picturesque winter sports and hiking resort lies at the junction of two major Alpine routes: the east–west Furka-Oberalp road and the north–south St Gotthard highway. From the top of Gemstock (2,961m/ 9,714ft), reached by cable car, you can see a remarkable 600 Alpine peaks. The town is bypassed by the 16km (10-mile) Gotthard road tunnel – the second-longest in the world – which links the cantons of Uri and Ticino.

Lake Geneva region

Geneva is Switzerland's best-known city – where so many major international treaties have been signed, and home to the headquarters of several global organisations. Decisions made here are often of world importance, made in an idyllic setting by the lake with a stunning Alpine backdrop. Charming, elegant and heavily influenced by neighbouring France, Geneva is the nation's most cosmopolitan city, celebrated for its watchmaking and banking, and second only in size to Zurich.

The surrounding countryside (part of the canton of Vaud) affords grandiose lake and Alpine vistas, some of the nation's most famous vineyards, lush forests, cornfields, tiny beaches and ancient stone villages. Lake Geneva (Lac Léman in French) has been described as the most elegant lake in the world, and a cruise along the shoreline reveals glimpses of castles, palatial residences,

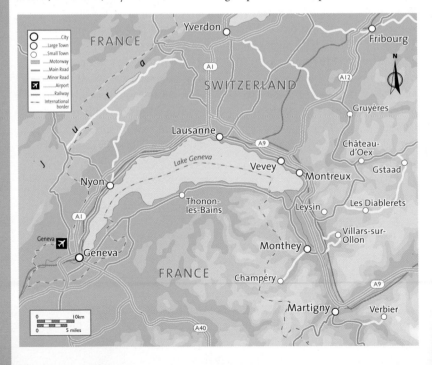

The enormous Jet d'Eau, icon of Geneva

and alluring Belle Époque resorts. Montreux-Vevey-Lavaux, at the eastern end of the lake, is also known as the Swiss Riviera. Like its French counterpart, over the years it has been a magnet for the rich and famous, including such cultural greats as Victor Hugo, Ernest Hemingway, Gustave Courbet, Graham Greene, Noel Coward and Charlie Chaplin.

The Swiss Riviera marks the departure point for luxury GoldenPass Belle Époque panoramic train rides to the Bernese Oberland, and it takes less than one hour to reach the nearest ski resorts in the Alpes Vaudoises. Les Diablerets is the most snow-sure resort, with its glacier skiing, while the traditional villages of Leysin, Villars and Château-d'Oex offer a large variety of year-round activities from paragliding, trekking and mountain biking to snowshoeing, skiing and sledding.

Genève (Geneva)

Geneva is Switzerland's grandest city, and one of the safest in the world. It is undeniably elegant, efficient, a little staid, but above all, thoroughly cosmopolitan. Over 250 international organisations are based here, including the World Health Organization (WHO), the International Red Cross, the World Meteorological Organization, and the United Nations European headquarters. Idyllically located between the Alps and the Jura mountains in the Rhône Valley, at the southwestern corner of Lake Geneva, Geneva is only connected to Switzerland by the lake and a narrow corridor. Otherwise, it is surrounded by French territory, and the city's unmistakeable French influence can be seen in its architecture (mansard roofs, iron balconies), its pavement cafés, its celebrated gastronomic tradition and its typically French signs.

Its Old Town is the most historic district with its quaint, steep streets, fountains and squares, and a fascinating mix of Gothic, Renaissance and 18th-century architecture. The city has a long and eventful history, reflected in its many museums and galleries.

Geneva is dotted with magnificent buildings: ten castles, countless parks, world-class museums, and gracious tree-shaded lakeside promenades. The River Rhône and the lake split the city into the artistic *rive gauche* (left bank), with the quaint, cobbled Old Town at its heart and some major shopping streets, and the grandiose *rive droite* (right bank), defined by major international organisations and attractive parks. Geneva is a shopper's paradise, known not only for its upmarket fashion boutiques, its watch and jewellery shops, but also for the small galleries and quirky boutiques of the Old Town. The main shopping area is in the Rues Basses (Lower Town), between the Old Town and the lake. Le Paquis is one of the most elegant districts, with its haute couture boutiques and banks. South of the city, the attractive 17th-century suburb of Carouge is a popular destination, brimming with arts, antiques and fashion shops.

The city is easy to explore, thanks to a comprehensive tram and bus network. To get your bearings, consider one of the tourist office's audio-guided tours, a 35-minute ride on Le Mini-train de Genève (*Mar–Dec departures from quai du Mont-Blanc*), or a 40-minute tram tour (*May–Oct from places du Rhône*). Join locals promenading along the quays, past the city's verdant parks. The most scenic section is from Parc de Mon Repos on the *rive droite* to the Parc des Eaux-Vives on the *rive gauche*. Look out also for the sensational Jardin Botanique (Botanical

LAKE GENEVA

The most romantic way to explore the Lake Geneva region is by boat. There are plenty of options: board the paddle steamer from Geneva to Lausanne; catch a small solar-powered ferry between Lutry, Pully and Lausanne; hire a sailing boat; enjoy a sunset cruise or a fondue dinner cruise; or opt for a memorable day trip embracing all the main sights, including the gentrified French town of Évian, Château de Chillon and the glamorous resorts of Vevey and Montreux.

See www.cgn.ch for more information.

A paddle steamer on Lake Geneva

Garden) – one of Geneva's most visited sights – and Parc la Grange, the nation's best rose garden.

Lake Geneva is the 'blue lung' of the city. Hardly surprisingly, sailing is the most popular sport, and in summer, kiosks line the quays hiring out small boats. Board a paddle steamer to cruise further afield (*see opposite*), past celebrity residences and some of Switzerland's most celebrated vineyards, or simply use the small *mouettes genevoise* boats that shuttle visitors from one quay to another.
Geneva Tourism, rue du Mont-Blanc 18. Tel: (022) 909 70. www.geneve-tourisme.ch. Open: mid-June–Aug Mon 10am–6pm, Tue–Sun 9am–6pm; Sept–mid-June Mon 10am–6pm, Tue–Sat 9am–6pm.

Musée Ariana

Housed in an Italian Renaissance building, this is one of Europe's top porcelain, glass and pottery museums with artefacts spanning seven centuries. It is also the headquarters of the International Academy of Ceramics.
Avenue de la Paix 10. Tel: (022) 418 54 50. Open: Wed–Mon 10am–5pm. Free admission. Bus Nos: 8, 28, F, V, Z (Appia).

Musée d'Art et d'Histoire – MAH (Museum of Art and History)

Geneva's most important museum contains everything from prehistoric relics, ancient Greek statuary and Etruscan pottery to medieval furniture and stained glass, Swiss watches, applied arts, and paintings from Rembrandt to Claude Monet.
Rue Charles Galland 2. Tel: (022) 418 26 00. www.ville-ge.ch/mah. Open: Tue–Sun 10am–5pm. Free admission. Bus Nos: 3, 5 (Athénée).

GENEVA INTERNATIONAL MOTOR SHOW

Europe's largest and most prestigious car exhibition – the International Motor Show – is staged at the Palexpo exhibition centre at Geneva Airport each March (*www.salon-auto.ch*). During the rest of the year, the International Automobile Museum features classic cars, prototypes, racing machines and motorcycles.
Palexpo, Grand-Saconnex. Tel: (022) 788 84 84. Open: Wed–Fri 1.30–6.30pm, Sat & Sun 10am–6pm. Admission charge.

The medieval Old Town in Lausanne

Musée d'Art Moderne et Contemporain – MAMCO (Museum of Modern and Contemporary Art)

This modern art museum is housed in a former factory building and showcases art, sculpture, photography and video installations from the past four decades, gathered from 40 private Swiss collections.

Rue des Vieux Grenadiers 10. Tel: (022) 320 61 22. www.mamco.ch. Open: Tue–Fri noon–6pm, Sat & Sun 11am–6pm. Admission charge. Bus No: 1 (École de Médicine).

Musée International de la Croix-Rouge et du Croissant-Rouge (Red Cross and Red Crescent Museum)

Located within the headquarters of the International Committee of the Red Cross, this museum portrays the history of modern conflict, and the role of the Red Cross in providing humanitarian aid in times of crisis since its foundation in 1864, through vivid, interactive displays and multimedia. The fascinating 'Today' area provides up-to-date news of current conflicts and world disasters.

Avenue de la Paix 17. Tel: (022) 748 95 25. www.micr.org. Open: Wed–Mon 10am–5pm. Admission charge. Bus No: 8 (Appia).

Musée Patek Philippe (Patek Philippe Museum)

No other Swiss town has been associated with the luxury watch industry as much as Geneva, and the Patek Philippe Company is among the world's most revered watchmakers. The museum contains fascinating audio-visual displays and over 2,000

objects relating to time, split into the 'Antiques Collection' (European, Swiss and Genevese watches from the 16th to the 19th centuries) and the 'Patek Philippe Collection', showcasing products from the company's foundation in 1839 to the present, and including the Calibre 89 – '*the most complicated watch in the world*'.
Rue des Vieux Grenadiers 7. Tel: (022) 807 09 10. www.patekmuseum.com. Open: Tue–Fri 2–6pm, Sat 10am–6pm. Admission charge.
Bus Nos: 1, 4 (École-de-Médecine); Tram Nos: 12, 13 (Plainpalais).

Palais des Nations (Palace of Nations)
The Palais des Nations was built in the 1930s to house the League of Nations, an organisation established to prevent a recurrence of war on the scale of World War I, but now defunct. Since 1966, it has been home to the UNOG (United Nations Office at Geneva). Compelling hour-long tours in any of the UN's official languages (passport required) include a visit to the Assembly Hall, the Court of Honour, the Council Chamber and a small philatelic museum with stamps dating back to the League of Nations.
Parc de l'Ariana, avenue de la Paix 14. Tel: (022) 917 48 96. www.unog.ch. Open: July & Aug 10am–5pm; Apr–June & Sept–Oct 10am–noon & 2–4pm; Nov–Mar Mon–Fri 10am–noon & 2–4pm. Admission charge.
Bus Nos: 8, 28, F, V, Z (Appia); Bus Nos: 5, 11, 14 (Nations).

Lausanne

The lively, youthful and cosmopolitan 'Olympic City' of Lausanne is built on three steep hills on the banks of Lake Geneva. As the headquarters of the International Olympic Committee (IOC) since 1915, as well as another 15 international sports federations, it is indeed a 'sportsville', with over 330 active sports clubs, ranging from water sports on the lake to cross-country skiing and hiking in the surrounding countryside. With a plethora of stylish shops, atmospheric restaurants, theatres and the nation's best nightlife outside Zurich, the Lausannois certainly know how to play hard, giving the city an undeniably laid-back atmosphere.

The medieval heart of the city comes as a surprise amid the modern metropolis, with its twisting lanes, pretty squares and wooden covered stairways, centred on the cobbled place de la Palud. Its cathedral is its crowning glory – Switzerland's most impressive Gothic monument. Lausanne is the last city to keep alive the tradition of the nightwatchman who calls the hour from the tower every night. Above the cathedral, the squat 14th-century château marks the highest tip of the Old Town. The up-and-coming neighbourhood of Le Flon, nearby, was once a quarter of merchants and traders. Today, its warehouses have been transformed into alternative cafés, experimental theatres and trendy dance clubs at the heart of the city's thriving (*Cont. on p72*)

Walk: Geneva's Old Town and quays

No visit to Geneva is complete without strolling by the lake and exploring the steep, cobbled streets of the picturesque Old Town, with its ancient houses, small boutiques and lively cafés and restaurants.

Start at quai Gustave Ador, on the shore of the lake, beside the Jardin Anglais. Allow 1¹/₂ hours.

1 Jardin Anglais (English Garden)

The English Garden is best known for its working flower clock, made up of over 6,500 flowers. Across the lake, the most celebrated city symbol, the Jet d'Eau (known affectionately to the Genevese as the *jeddo*) dates from 1891, and pumps 500 litres (132 gallons) of water per second a staggering 138m (452ft) into the air.

Proceed across the Pont du Mont-Blanc (Mont-Blanc Bridge) over the River Rhône at the mouth of the lake and turn left along the elegant quai des Bergues.

2 Île Rousseau

This small island (accessed by the narrow Pont des Bergues), with its ducks and statue of Geneva's celebrated philosopher, Jean-Jacques Rousseau, was once part of the city's defences.

Continue along quai des Bergues to place St-Gervais. Turn left to cross the river past the Tour-de-l'Île.

3 Tour-de-l'Île

This tower is all that remains of a medieval bishops' château, once used as a prison and place of execution by the Counts of Savoy.

Head south along rue de la Monnaie. Enter the Old Town up cobbled rue de la Cité. Turn right at the top into rue de la Tertasse, and descend steeply to place Neuve.

4 Place Neuve

This elegant, spacious square is Geneva's cultural nerve centre, containing the Grand Théâtre, the Conservatory of Music, the Musée Rath art gallery, and a statue of General Dufour, co-founder of the Red Cross. In the Parc des Bastions, an impressive 100m (328ft) Mur des Réformateurs lines the city ramparts. Created in 1917, it features the four Genevese reformers (John Calvin, John Knox, Théodore de Bèze and Guillaume Farel), alongside Cromwell, Luther, Zwingli and the Pilgrim Fathers.

Exit place Neuve up the steep rampe de la Treille and turn left through a classical archway down rue Henri-Fazy to the Hôtel de Ville.

5 Hôtel de Ville (Town Hall)

The Red Cross was founded in this 16th-century Town Hall in 1864.
Descend rue du Puits-Saint-Pierre beside the 17th-century arcaded Arsenal. Turn right at rue Otto-Barblan to Cour de St-Pierre.

6 Cathédrale de St-Pierre (St Peter's Cathedral)

The Cathédrale de St-Pierre was built between 1150 and 1232 on the site of a Roman temple. View the 4th-century sculptures and mosaics in the crypt. Over the years, the cathedral was enlarged and, in 1536, locals voted to make it Protestant. The north tower affords spectacular views of the region.
Head left on exiting the cathedral. Cross place de la Taconnerie, then turn left down rue de l'Hôtel de Ville to place du Bourg-de-Four.

7 Place du Bourg-de-Four

This photogenic square is one of Geneva's most historic: former Roman forum, medieval marketplace, site of the Palais de Justice and Jean-Jacques Rousseau's birthplace (at No 40). It is also the geographical and spiritual heart of the Old Town, with plenty of pavement bars and cafés for refreshment.
Return downhill (via rue de la Fontaine) to the lake and the Jardin Anglais.

Walk: Geneva's Old Town and quays

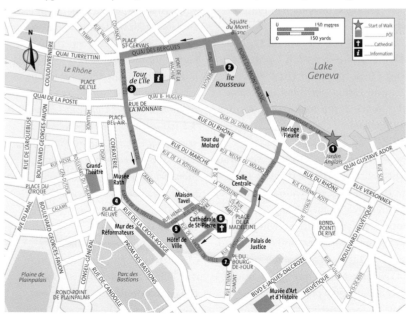

counterculture. The waterfront district of Ouchy is graced with manicured floral parks and glitzy marinas, where locals and energetic inline skaters take in the air along tree-lined waterside promenades stretching from Geneva to Lutry. The city's main museum, the Musée Olympique, is also located here. *Lausanne Tourisme, place de la Gare 9. Tel: (021) 613 73 73. www.lausanne-tourisme.ch. Open: 9am–7pm.*

Musée Cantonal des Beaux-Arts

This major gallery contains an impressive collection of Swiss art from the 18th to the 20th century, including many Vaudois artists. It is housed in the neo-Renaissance Palais de Rumine, where the Treaty of Lausanne was signed in 1923, finalising the partitioning of the Ottoman Empire after World War I.
Place de la Riponne 6. Tel: (021) 316 34 45. www.beaux-arts.vd.ch. Open: Tue & Wed 11am–6pm, Thur 11am–8pm, Fri–Sun 11am–5pm. Admission charge. Bus Nos: 1, 2 (Rue Neuve); Bus Nos: 5, 6, 8 (Riponne).

Musée Olympique (Olympic Museum)

This stunning lakeside museum is the world's leading centre of information and research on the Olympic movement and its ideals, highlighting the union of sport, art and culture, and showing the most memorable moments of Olympic history through exciting 3-D audio-visual presentations and state-of-the-art special effects.

Quai d'Ouchy 1. Tel: (021) 621 65 11. www.olympic.org. Open: 9am–6pm. Closed: Mon & Nov–Mar. Admission charge. Bus No: 8 (Musée Olympique).

SWISS RIVIERA
Montreux

Thanks to its spectacular location and mild climate, stylish Montreux was already a popular health resort by the end of the 19th century, and today its many *belle époque* hotels and mansions bear witness to its heyday. Montreux has long attracted writers, musicians, poets and actors, from Jean-Jacques Rousseau and Ernest Hemingway to Igor Stravinsky, and even Freddie Mercury, whose statue graces the palm-lined lakeside promenade. Follow in the footsteps of the famous all the way to Vevey in a self-guided walk (maps are available from the tourist office).

However, the spa town is perhaps best known for the Montreux International Jazz Festival in July, the most prestigious jazz festival in the world (*see p19*).
Montreux Tourisme, place de l'Eurovision. Tel: (0848) 86 84 84. www.montreux-vevey.com. Open: Mon–Fri 9am–6pm, Sat & Sun 9.30am–5pm (summer); Mon–Fri 9am–noon & 1–5.30pm, Sat & Sun 10am–2pm (winter).

Château de Chillon

It takes 45 minutes to walk from Montreux along the lake to Château de Chillon, a beautiful medieval castle built on Roman foundations on a rock beside the lake, and one of

Switzerland's most visited sights. First owned by the bishop of Sion, then the medieval seat of the Counts of Savoy, it was immortalised by countless artists and writers, including English poet Lord Byron, in *The Prisoner of Chillon*.

Tel: (021) 966 89 10. www.chillon.ch. Open: Jan & Feb, Nov & Dec 10am–5pm; Mar & Oct 9.30am–6pm; Apr–Sept 9am–7pm (last entry 1 hour before closing). Admission charge. Bus No: 1 (Chillon).

Vevey

Former residents of this elegant lakeside spa resort include Jean-Jacques Rousseau and Charlie Chaplin. The latter lived here for 25 years in the Manoir de Ban, which in 2010 will open as a museum in his honour. Stroll along the gracious promenade (with its Chaplin statue) and browse the quality boutiques of the Old Town selling wine, cheese, chocolate, arts and crafts and antiques. The market hall here was built following a donation by local businessman Henri Nestlé. Modelled on Paris's Halles, it was constructed from steel from the same smithy that supplied Gustave Eiffel for his tower. There is a food market in the place du Marché every Tuesday and Saturday morning.

Montreux-Vevey Tourisme, Grande-Place 29. Tel: (0848) 86 84 84. www.montreux-vevey.com. Open: Mon–Fri 9am–6pm, Sat 8.30am–12.30pm (summer; until 1pm mid-July–Aug); Mon–Fri

9am–noon & 1–5.30pm, Sat 9am–noon (winter).

Alimentarium (Food Museum)

Nestlé's headquarters have been in Vevey since 1814, and their fascinating food museum analyses various aspects of food in a lively and interactive way, with hands-on activities, and even an opportunity to cook.

Quai Perdonnet, Vevey. Tel: (021) 924 41 11. www.alimentarium.ch. Open: Tue–Sun 10am–6pm. Admission charge.

Musée Historique de Vevey (Historial Museum)

This beautiful 16th-century mansion documents the region's glorious past, together with a large section devoted to

Château de Chillon

the massive Fête des Vignerons (Winegrowers Festival), which takes place here every 25 years.

Rue du Château 2. Tel: (021) 921 07 22. www.museehistoriquevevey.ch. Open: Apr–Oct Tue–Sun 11am–5pm; Nov–Mar Tue–Sun 2–5pm. Admission charge.

Musée Suisse du Jeu (Swiss Games Museum)

This charming museum, situated in a small lakeside castle, is great fun especially for children, with its various interactive games.

Château de la Tour-de-Peilz. Tel: (021) 977 23 00. www.museedujeu.com. Open: Tue–Sun 11am–5.30pm. Admission charge.

ALPES VAUDOISES
Château-d'Oex

Nestling between Gruyère and Gstaad, this traditional mountain village in the beautiful Vaudois mountains is a popular ski resort with families with its superb runs, permanent slalom, toboggan runs and snow park.

However, it is best known as the world's hot-air ballooning capital and the start point of the Breitling Orbiter III, the first successful circumnavigation of the globe by balloon in 1999. Every January, Château-d'Oex hosts Europe's largest ballooning festival. The Espace Ballon Museum traces the history of this eccentric mode of travel (*Tel: (026) 924 22 20. www.ballonchateaudoex.ch. Open: mid-Dec–Feb, late June–mid-Sept*

and school holidays 10am–noon & 2–6pm; rest of year 2–6pm. Admission charge).

Château-d'Oex Tourisme, La Place, Château-d'Oex. Tel: (026) 924 25 25. www.chateau-doex.ch

Les Diablerets

Les Diablerets maintains a traditional village atmosphere with its wooden chalets and majestic mountain scenery, despite being a modern ski resort that has the largest ski area in the Lake Geneva region (combined with Villars-Gryon and Gstaad). The resort is located at the foot of the only glacier in the region; Glacier 3000 (*www.glacier3000.ch*) is one of Switzerland's newest ski areas, with brilliant skiing and snowboarding from

Balloon festival at Château-d'Oex

October until May, and the longest piste in the Alpes Vaudoises, at 14km (8½ miles). There are plenty of activities for non-skiers, including a winter hiking route, dog sledding, snow-bus routes, tobogganing and in summer, hiking, mountain biking and climbing trails. And be sure to take the state-of-the-art cable car to the summit for dazzling Alpine panoramas from the sleek, futuristic restaurant Botta 3000, designed by Swiss architect Mario Botta (*see p56*).
Diablerets Tourisme, rue de la Gare.
Tel: (24) 492 33 58. www.diablerets.ch

Leysin

High above Lake Geneva and the Rhône Valley, the trendy resort of Leysin is one of Switzerland's snowboarding capitals. Its Freestyle SnowPark at the foot of the highest peak, La Berneuse, is setting new global standards for boarding, with its snow obstacles and challenging superpipe (140m/460ft long, with a gradient of −20°). Leysin is undeniably a resort of high-adrenalin sports, from ice-karting in winter on the ice rink to year-round paragliding. It also offers the only tobogganing park in Switzerland with long, carved snow chutes built of packed snow, similar to a bobsleigh track (*see p163*). In summer, there are nine specialist graded bike routes on the slopes of the Berneuse; over 160km (100 miles) of hiking trails; and two *via ferrata* (metal ladders in the rock face), giving novices

a taste of rock climbing, but without the ropes. Alternatively, simply relax on the beautiful sun terrace of the famous Kuklos revolving restaurant (*see p163*).
Leysin Tourisme, place Large.
Tel: (024) 494 33 00. www.leysin.ch

Villars-sur-Ollon

Villars is situated at 1,350m (4,429ft) above sea level on a natural balcony in the heart of the Alpes Vaudoises, in a sunny southern location facing Mont Blanc, the Dents du Midi and the Rhône Valley. Despite its low altitude, it offers excellent skiing, especially for beginners, intermediates and families, with a good ski school. In summer months, the resort offers a wealth of leisure and sporting activities, including an 18-hole Alpine golf course.
Villars Tourisme, rue Centrale.
Tel: (024) 495 32 32. www.villars.ch

LAVAUX VINEYARDS

Wine production in Vaud dates from Roman times. The terraced Lavaux vineyards cling to the steep slopes of Lake Geneva, and such beautifully preserved golden stone villages as Rivaz and St Saphorin, where the winegrowers live and press their grapes, provide a host of scenic walks and wine-tasting opportunities in the local *caveaux* (wine cellars). There's a 32km (20-mile) 'Lavaux Wine Trail', stretching from Lausanne's Olympic Museum to Villeneuve at the easternmost tip of the lake, while the tiny *Lavaux Express* tourist train winds through the vineyards from the lakeside village of Lutry via Aran to Grandvaux, or from Cully to Rièx, Epesses and Dézaley (*Open: late Mar–Oct. www.lavauxexpress.ch*).

Chocolate

Swiss chocolate is the finest in the world, and the nation's greatest pride, alongside their cheese, railways and mountains. The Swiss themselves are passionate chocoholics, consuming an average 10.3kg (22¾lb) a head per year, making them the world's largest consumers of chocolate. In the towns and cities, daily life without chocolate would be unimaginable. Hot chocolate is served in many cafés, especially in winter, and chocolate shops abound, luring in passers-by with their tantalising window displays and the sweet smell of melted chocolate.

Chocolate history

Switzerland has a long tradition of chocolatiers producing hand-filled luxury chocolates, rich in cocoa butter. In 1819, François-Louis Cailler began Swiss production in Vevey, having acquired the skill and chocolate from Italian confectioners, followed shortly after by Philippe Suchard in Neuchâtel. Both produced dark, bitter, plain chocolate. However, the real Swiss breakthrough was the invention of solid milk chocolate in 1875, by Daniel Peters in Vevey, initially using the powdered milk that his neighbour Henri Nestlé had recently invented, and later condensed milk, to create a rich, creamy-tasting chocolate. In 1897, Rodolphe Lindt created 'conching' (a mixing process to produce smooth, liquid chocolate) in Bern.

The first ever chocolate factory – the Cailler Factory at Broc – was opened in 1898. Bernese confectioner Jean Tobler made further history in 1909 with the first chocolate patent – a triangular-shaped bar called

An appetising display

An old chocolate factory in Bern

Bellet 7, Broc. Tel: (026) 921 51 51.
*www.cailler.ch. Open: Apr–Oct daily
9.30am–4pm. Free admission).*

Top chocolatiers

The most famous Swiss chocolatiers
are Sprüngli and Teuscher. For the
ultimate chocolate experiences, visit
Sprüngli's flagship store at Paradeplatz
in Zurich, where the world-famous
pralinés, truffes du jour and other
specialities are lovingly handmade
daily according to traditional recipes,
or eat champagne truffles at
Teuscher's main store in Zurich's
Old Town. Look out also for
another Swiss speciality – seasonal
confectionery and novelty chocolate
forms: chocolate flowers in spring;
chocolate chestnuts in autumn;
chocolate bears in Bern; chocolate
watches in the Jura; and even
chocolate dustbins in Geneva.

Toblerone, containing honey and
almonds, and allegedly inspired by the
shape of the Matterhorn. Finally, in
1913, Jules Séchaud of Montreux
developed a technique for making
chocolate shells filled with other
confections, putting Switzerland at
the forefront of chocolate
manufacture. Nestlé's Cailler factory
still exists at Broc and is just one of
several manufacturers offering
tastings and guided factory tours
(including SchokoLand Alprose near
Lugano, *www.alprose.ch*, and
Schoggi Land near St Gallen,
www.schoggi-land.ch). At the end of
the Cailler tour there are heaps of
bite-sized chocolates to try. Signs
explain how a professional chocolate
taster assesses quality, but most
people just opt for quantity (*rue Jules*

THE CHOCOLATE TRAIN

If you have a sweet tooth, consider a day
aboard the *Chocolate Train*, with its *Belle
Époque* and panoramic carriages. Follow
the Swiss Riviera from Montreux then
climb above Lake Geneva through Gruyères
(to visit the castle and cheese factory) then
on to the Nestlé-Cailler factory at Broc,
before returning to Montreux.
*Tel: (+41) 840 245 245 (from abroad); 0900
245 245 (from Switzerland). www.mob.ch.
Open: June, Sept–Oct Mon, Wed & Thur,
July–Aug Mon–Fri. Reservations essential;
tickets available at any train station.*

Valais

The canton of Valais has the highest mountains in Switzerland, and the longest glacier and highest vineyards in Europe. It is a region of rugged mountain scenery and picturesque villages that act as a year-round magnet for sport- and nature-lovers.

With more 4,000m (13,124ft) peaks than anywhere in Switzerland, Valais is an outstanding snow region. As soon as the first snow begins to fall, people flock from all over Europe to the region's legendary ski resorts.

There are over 120 winter sports resorts in Valais alone, ranging from the simple charm of Grimentz and St-Luc in the Val d'Anniviers to the fashionable splendour of Verbier and Zermatt.

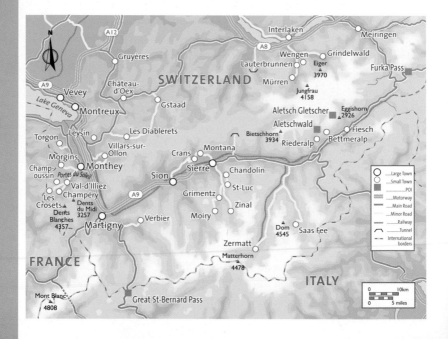

The instantly recognisable Matterhorn

French-speaking Verbier is one of the finest ski areas in Europe, combining rustic appeal with some of the most challenging runs and the best lift-served off-piste skiing in the Alps, not to mention its exuberant après-ski. But no ski resort is as impressive as glamorous German-speaking Zermatt, with the majestic Matterhorn – the nation's most powerful image – as its backdrop.

In summer, the Valaisan landscape is straight out of picture books, with lush meadows ablaze with Alpine herbs and flowers, verdant hillsides dotted with ancient barns and chalets, icy blue lakes, dense fragrant forests of pine and larch, and a plethora of giant, snow-capped peaks all around. The flora and fauna are exceptional, and keen-eyed walkers will enjoy spotting marmots, ibex, chamois (horned antelope), redstarts and golden eagles.

While skiers and hikers enjoy the high-altitude activities, down in the valleys there are some of the world's most luxurious mountain hotels; Alpine villages of dark brown, sun-worn wooden barns and chalets; and welcoming historic towns with a host of museums, galleries, folkloric and cultural activities, not to mention the little-known but superb regional wines and local gastronomy.

Mountains

With 60 per cent of Switzerland covered by Alps, and the Jura mountains occupying a further 10 per cent, it is little wonder that the Swiss love hiking. They are joined by 120 million visitors annually, keen to enjoy some of Europe's best Alpine walking, unparalleled vistas and an astonishingly wide range of mountain wildlife.

Hiking

There are over 60,000km (37,200 miles) of designated hiking paths in Switzerland, which are clearly marked

The majestic ibex

and colour-coded according to difficulty. The majority are straightforward and marked by yellow signs, which often indicate the walking time to the next destination. Mountain paths are indicated by red-and-white-striped markers painted on prominent trees and rocks along the route and are generally more advanced, suitable only for people with good fitness levels and sturdy, non-slip footwear. The higher Alpine routes are indicated by white-blue-white marks, and should only be tackled by experienced mountain walkers, accompanied by a mountain guide and with specialist equipment.

Some of the best hiking is in the Jungfrau region and in Valais, with its classic chocolate-box scenery and the largest number of peaks exceeding 4,000m (13,124ft) in Switzerland. Schweizer Wanderwegen (Swiss Hiking Federation; *www.swisshiking.ch*) produces a series of excellent hiking maps and organises guided walking tours.

Mountain huts

As camping rough is formally prohibited by Swiss law, one popular overnight option for hikers is to stay

Tiny, white stars of edelweiss

crocuses and violet-blue gentians in spring, followed by the bright pink *Alpenrosen*, yellow-and-white glacier buttercups and rare edelweiss – the unofficial Swiss national flower, with its tiny, star-shaped, white flowers.

in a mountain hut. The Schweizer Alpen-club (Swiss Alpine Club) maintains around 150 huts for overnight stays, offering simple and cheap, often dormitory-style, accommodation. Facilities vary from hut to hut – some have a hot meal and a hot shower, others are more basic, unstaffed and rely on your honesty for payment. For details of each hut, see *www.sac-cas.ch*

Flora
The fragile ecosystem of the Alps shelters some rare and magnificent plants. The treeline in the Alps is usually around 2,000m (6,561ft), with conifers and red spruce on lower slopes giving way to Arolla pine and larch higher up, then bushes and scrub followed by Alpine meadows. Alpine meadows are in bloom from April to July. Look out for early white

Fauna
If you are lucky while hiking, you may spot red deer, chamois or ibex, a mountain goat with huge curved and ridged horns. Ibex are one of a major, and so far successful, re-colonisation programme of endangered animals into their original habitat, together with the pointy-eared European lynx, the mountain hare, ermine, weasel, fox, wolf and even the European brown bear. Look out also for small grey marmots, which live in underground burrows on the slopes, and who can often be heard whistling to signal imminent danger – one whistle for airborne predators, more for ground predators.

In the skies, the rare European kestrel, golden eagle and bearded vulture (*see p119*) can occasionally be spotted. Less impressive, but equally rare, are the *Alpendohle*, related to the crow, with black feathers and a yellow beak, the noisy nutcracker with white and brown speckled plumage, and the chicken-like rock ptarmigan.

Aletsch Gletscher (Aletsch Glacier)

The Aletsch Gletscher is the largest glacier in the Alps, a remarkable 23.6km (14½-mile) long ice sheet resembling a massive icy motorway that winds dramatically down from the Jungfrau in the Bernese Oberland. It is the highlight of the Jungfrau-Aletsch-Bietschhorn UNESCO World Natural Heritage Site, and is fringed by the Aletschwald, one of Europe's highest larch and mountain pine forests, and home to Switzerland's oldest trees.

Three charming, car-free hamlets (Riederalp, Bettmeralp and Fiescheralp) nestle near the southern rim of the glacier, with an interlinking network of hiking trails, cable cars and lifts. In winter, these hamlets join forces as a popular ski area. During summer, the Eggishorn (2,926m/9,600ft), reached by cable car from Fiesch, offers the best viewpoint of the glacier. From here, there is a spectacular four-hour UNESCO high-altitude ridge trail to Bettmerhorn (for experienced hikers only), where an interactive 'Ice World' display provides a fascinating glimpse into the world of glaciers.
www.aletsch.ch

Crans-Montana

This chic twin resort attracts moneyed Swiss and international visitors to its sunny slopes, perched on a plateau overlooking the Rhône Valley and the highest Alpine peaks from Mont Blanc to the Matterhorn.

The main summer activities here are hiking, mountain biking and golf, with some of the nation's top courses,

The Aletsch Glacier, largest in the Alps

including the Severiano Ballesteros 18-hole course and the Jack Nicklaus, Supercrans and Noas 9-hole courses. In winter, it becomes a prestigious ski resort, with 140km (87 miles) of mostly intermediate-level pistes linking the Plaine Morte glacier to the resorts. There are good children's facilities, and a sophisticated après-ski scene.
Crans-Montana Tourisme. Tel: (027) 485 04 04. www.crans-montana.ch

Les Portes du Soleil (Gateway to the Sun)

During the 1960s, a group of friends in 14 villages created the 'Haute Route des Familles' (the original name of the Portes du Soleil), with the plan that everyone should be able to go from one valley to another on skis, irrespective of international borders. Today's Portes du Soleil straddles France and Switzerland, yet maintains the concept of border-free enjoyment of the mountains, and the original 14 villages have since grown to become popular resorts. Today, with over 650km (403 miles) of pistes, 206 ski lifts and 288 runs, Portes du Soleil is the largest international ski region in the world and, as long as you carry your passport, you can ski wherever you wish.

The two best-known resorts are the modern, snowboarding mecca of Avoriaz in France and the traditional resort of Champéry in Switzerland, set at the foot of the magnificent Dents du Midi and Dents Blanches mountains. The other Swiss resorts are Torgon,

You can ski freely in the Portes du Soleil

Morgins, Vall-d'Illiez, Champoussin and Les Crosets. Each has managed to preserve its traditional architecture and friendly village atmosphere.

The area is popular with nature-lovers and sports fanatics all year round. As well as skiing in winter, there is ice-diving, frozen-waterfall climbing, dog sledding, ice-skating and snowshoeing, while in summer popular activities include horse riding, golf, paragliding, mountaineering and trekking, with over 800km (497 miles) of hiking trails and 580km (360 miles) of mountain-bike trails.
Les Portes du Soleil.
Tel: +33 (0)4 50 73 32 54.
www.portesdusoleil.com

The revolving restaurant on Allalin, Saas Fee

Saas Fee

The German-speaking ski village of Saas Fee, with its impressive glacier, is known as the 'Pearl of the Alps' because it is located on a high plateau encircled by 13 peaks over 4,000m (13,124ft), including one of Switzerland's highest mountains, the Dom, at 4,545m (14,911ft). It also has the world's largest ice pavilion (*www.eispavillon.ch*) and the highest revolving restaurant at the 3,500m (11,482ft) Allalin peak.

Saas Fee offers superb, snow-sure skiing with 100km (62 miles) of pistes, children's facilities, and vivacious nightlife. The pedestrian village maintains its authentic Swiss atmosphere with its attractive Valaisan chalets and farmhouses. Tobogganing, husky-dog sledding and snowshoeing are also popular winter pursuits. In summer, it is a paradise for nature-lovers, with extensively marked hiking trails.

Saas Fee Tourismus. Tel: (027) 958 18 58. www.saas-fee.ch

Verbier

Well known for its seemingly limitless off-piste skiing and its lively après-ski scene, Verbier is one of the largest and most outstanding ski areas in the world. Set on a broad, sun-drenched plateau at the heart of Valais, it is a thriving modern ski town, although its chalet-style buildings lend it the charm of a large Alpine village.

Above the town, Verbier is linked to the neighbouring resorts of Thyon, Veysonnaz and Nendaz to form Les Quatre Vallées, creating a huge and varied ski paradise with 400km

(248 miles) of runs to suit all levels. Nendaz is especially family-friendly and Thyon is popular for snowboarders and freeriders. However, advanced skiers have the most fun in this vast winter playground, as Verbier offers some of the most challenging slopes in the Alps, including the vertiginous mogul fields of Mont-Fort and Chassoure and the notoriously steep couloirs and powder bowls of Tortin and Mont Gelé.

In summer, high-adrenalin sports such as downhill mountain biking, mountain climbing, paragliding, glacier hiking and rock climbing are popular, together with trekking and golf.

Verbier Tourisme, place Centrale, Verbier. Tel: (027) 775 38 88. www.verbier.ch, www.4vallees.ch

Zermatt

Picture postcard Zermatt is consistently ranked as one of the world's top five ski resorts. It is located in German-speaking Valais, and dominated by the mighty Matterhorn. From the top of the resort, it is possible to see a staggering 38 of Europe's 76 4,000m (13,124ft) high peaks.

The chalet-lined streets of this romantic, pedestrianised village are packed with beautiful boutiques, cosy bars, sophisticated restaurants and some of the Alps' most glamorous hotels. Transport is by horse-drawn carriage or electric taxi. Beside the church, the Matterhorn Museum reveals the story of Switzerland's most famous mountain, from its dramatic first ascent by Edward Whymper in 1865, and how the small farming community of Zermatt became an internationally famous and fashionable resort.

Kirchplatz 11. Tel: (027) 967 41 00. www.matterhornmuseum.ch. Open: Mid-Dec–Easter 3pm–7pm; Easter–June & Oct 2pm–6pm; July–Sept 11am–6pm. Closed Nov–mid-Dec.

The ski area links up with Cervinia in Italy to offer 313km (194 miles) of well-groomed pistes, although the best skiing is on the slopes of the Gornergrat, reached after a spectacular cogwheel train ride on Europe's highest open-air railway. Summer activities include fantastic walking trails, tennis, swimming, cycling, and summer skiing on one of Europe's largest glaciers. Zermatt is also the start point of the world famous *Glacier Express* (*see p110*).

Zermatt Tourismus, Bahnhofplatz 5. Tel: (027) 966 81 00. www.zermatt.ch

The Matterhorn looms over the Zermatt area

Drive: Val d'Anniviers

From the vineyards of the Rhône to the eternal snow of the Zinal glacier, explore this most beautiful of Valaisan valleys with its 'chocolate-box' villages and exceptional mountain trails.

Start at Sion. Allow at least one full day (longer if you wish to complete all the walks).

1 Sion

Located in the Rhône Valley, Sion is the capital of Valais and the nation's oldest town. The ruins of Château de Tourbillon atop one hill are surrounded by a well-preserved medieval old town, while the 12th-century Basilique de Valère on the opposite hill contains the world's oldest playable organ.

Take the A9 motorway along the Rhône Valley to Sierre.

2 Sierre

This gracious town lies at the heart of a magnificent wine-growing region, and it is possible to taste the local wines (Fendant and Dôle) in Renaissance Château de Villa. Sierre is also the venue of Vinea, the largest wine festival in Valais every September.

Take the second motorway exit from Sierre, and follow southbound signs to Val d'Anniviers. Zigzag steeply up towards Vissoie, then turn left towards St-Luc.

3 St-Luc

St-Luc is a typical Anniviard village – a beautiful, unspoiled cluster of wooden chalets and traditional farm buildings oozing authentic mountain charm. In winter, it is a popular ski resort for the locals, with great views of the Matterhorn. In summer, it has sensational walking.

Continue up to Chandolin.

4 Chandolin

At 2,000m (6,560ft), picturesque Chandolin is the highest year-round inhabited village in Europe, and affords spectacular views of the Rhône Valley and Crans-Montana opposite.

Retrace your steps to Vissoie and continue through the delightful hamlet of St-Jean, with its celebrated fondue restaurant (see p166), to Grimentz.

5 Grimentz

With its beautiful sun-darkened wooden chalets, this charming 'Village of Flowers' is so quaint it could almost be an open-air museum. There is a handful of cosy restaurants and it is a popular family ski resort in winter. *Continue on to Moiry.*

6 Barrage de Moiry

The Val de Moiry is known for its edelweiss and other lovely wild flowers. Walk up the valley, around the right-hand side of the azure-blue Lac de Moiry (Moiry Lake), to reach the beautifully situated Cabane de Moiry for a meal or to stay overnight (*allow 2½ hours*). *Return to Vissoie. Turn right to Zinal.*

7 Zinal

Explore inside the glacier at Zinal or choose from a wide variety of trails and excursions that lead into the surrounding mountains, including Lac d'Arpitetaz (2,400m/7,873ft, *allow 3–4 hours*) and the Cabane de Petit Mountet (2,886m/9,468ft, *allow 5 hours*), high above Zinal's glacier, with incredible panoramas en route.

Drive: Val d'Anniviers

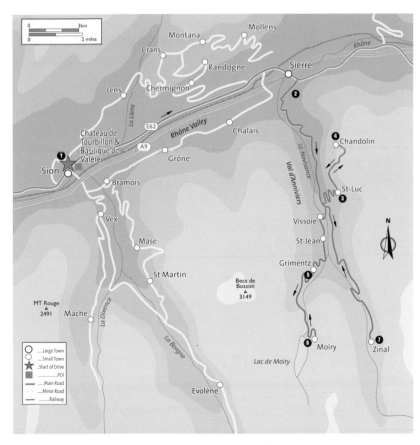

The Great St Bernard Pass

The pass

The Great St Bernard Pass linking Switzerland and Italy is the oldest mountain pass in history, running northeast–southwest through the Valaisan Alps. The Great St Bernard road tunnel plunges through the mountains at an elevation of 1,915m (6,282ft), while the smaller, historic road over the top of the pass is only open between June and September.

The hospice

The pass has endured a long and chequered history. It was first used in the Bronze Age (around 800 BC). In 390 BC, a Gaulish army crossed here to defeat Rome; Hannibal allegedly brought his elephants over the pass in 217 BC; and in 57 BC, Julius Caesar

The noble St Bernard

took this route to conquer Martigny. Emperor Augustus built the first road across the pass. However, centuries later in the early 10th century, Huns and Saracens rampaged through the region, terrorising travellers and demanding payment. Having seen so many grief-stricken travellers stripped of their belongings, Aosta's Archdeacon, Bernard of Menthon, decided in 1049 to create a hospice on the treacherous pass, at 2,469m (8,100ft), as a safe haven for travellers. Bernard was beatified shortly after his death in the 1080s.

Throughout the Middle Ages, the hospice provided shelter and food to travellers, and by 1817 around 20,000 people were crossing the pass annually. Remarkably, it still functions today as a shelter, nearly 1,000 years after its foundation. In 1923, Pope Pius XI declared St Bernard the patron saint of the Alps.

The dogs

In the early 18th century, dogs known as St Bernards were bred from the hunting and herding dogs of local farmers to be strong enough to handle deep snow and to rescue lost people. Once trained, they were sent out in

The Great Saint Bernard Pass

unaccompanied packs of two or three to search for lost pilgrims. Having dug the people out of the snow, one dog would lie on the victim to keep them warm while the other dog returned to the hospice to alert the monks. The most famous St Bernard was Barry, who saved over 40 lives, while the heaviest recorded was Benedictine at over 160kg (353lb). It is sometimes said that these gentle giants carried small casks of brandy around their necks, although the monks deny this, saying the image derives from an early painting.

St Bernard dogs have lived at the hospice ever since 1708. However, in 2004 the monks decided they could no longer maintain them *in situ*. Thankfully, a new museum and kennels has opened up in an ancient arsenal in Martigny, funded by a Genevois multimillionaire, in order to preserve the breed (*Musée et Chiens du Saint-Bernard, route du Levant 34, Martigny. Tel: (027) 720 49 20. www.museesaintbernard.ch. Open: 10am–6pm (June until 7pm; July–Aug until 10pm). Admission charge*). During summer months, the monks will look after some dogs in the kennel at the hospice – just to keep the tourists happy! *www.pays-du-saint-bernard.ch*

NAPOLEON'S DEBTS

In May 1800, Napoleon led 40,000 troops over the pass to Italy. He ran up a huge bill at the hospice of CHF40,000 before leaving. Fifty years later, the monks received CHF18,000 in part-payment. They had to wait until May 1984 for French president François Mitterrand to settle the bill.

Central Switzerland

This is one of Switzerland's most scenic regions, with classic vistas at every turn – geranium-clad medieval villages; crystal-clear blue lakes; lush flower-filled Alpine meadows; dense forests dotted with wooden chalets; and snow-capped mountains. The entire area is steeped in history. After all, this is William Tell country, where the Swiss Confederation was founded over 700 years ago.

Luzern is one of the most beautiful and most visited Swiss destinations – a perfect blend of history, architecture, scenery and culture. It is also an ideal base for excursions into the surrounding countryside, located at the northern edge of Lake Luzern, which forms part of the impressive Vierwaldstättersee (Lake of the Four Cantons).

The Vierwaldstättersee is situated at the meeting point of four cantons (Luzern, Uri, Unterwalden and Schwyz). It is the fourth-largest lake in Switzerland at 39km (24 miles) long and 3km (1¾ miles) wide, and its numerous genteel shoreline towns and villages are connected by the world's largest fleet of paddle steamers. The lake's slopes are a walkers' paradise,

Tour boat on Lake Luzern

with well-signposted trails. The most famous hike in the region is situated at the southernmost part of the Vierwaldstättersee around Urnersee; the Weg der Schweiz (Swiss Path) was designed in 1991 to celebrate the 700th anniversary of the Swiss Confederation here. Each section of the walk represents the individual cantons of Switzerland in the order that they joined the Confederation. The length of each canton's stretch represents the number of people living in that canton.

Cable cars and mountain railways in the region offer easy access to the steep upper slopes and to such mountain peaks as Rigi and Pilatus with their astounding 360-degree Alpine panoramas, while the celebrated St Gotthard Pass scales the heights between north and south – German-speaking and Italian-speaking Switzerland.

See pp94–5 for Tour

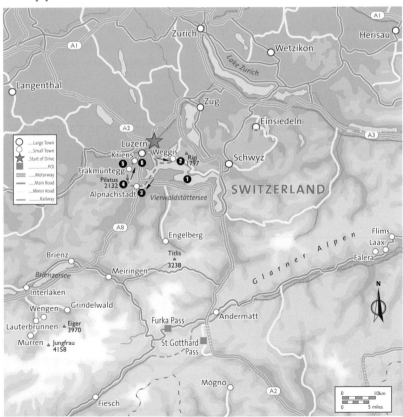

Luzern

With its extraordinary blend of lakes, mountains, culture, folklore, architecture and history, the beautiful city of Luzern (Lucerne in French), located at the very heart of the nation, is Switzerland at its picturesque best. A medieval town made famous as a stylish resort in the 19th century, it remains hugely popular today, located at the gateway to the high Alps, on the northern edge of the Vierwaldstättersee, and framed by the majestic peaks of Rigi and Pilatus.

The most attractive district is the medieval quarter, characterised by quaint cobbled streets, historical monuments, fortifications and ancient churches, set against the clear blue waters of Lake Luzern. The early 14th-century Kapellbrücke (Chapel Bridge) is Europe's oldest covered wooden footbridge, and the most photographed

The Kapellbrücke in Luzern

building in Switzerland. Heavily restored since a fire in 1993, many of its original Renaissance wall paintings have since been reproduced. Walk along the medieval ramparts for spectacular views over the ancient rooftops to the lake and mountains beyond. The most scenic stretch is from Wachtturm to the Zytturm, which has the city's oldest clock. Bizarrely, it chimes one minute before all the others in town.
Luzern Tourismus, Bahnhofstrasse 3. Tel: (041) 227 17 17. www.luzern.org

Gletschergarten (Glacier Garden)

This intriguing museum traces the geological history of the region from 20 million years ago through to the glacier world of the Great Ice Age 20,000 years ago.
Denkmalstrasse 4. Tel: (041) 410 43 40. www.gletschergarten.ch. Open: Apr–Oct 9am–6pm, Nov–Mar 10am–5pm. Admission charge.

KKL Kunstmuseum (Art Museum)

Best known for its traditions and folklore, Luzern has recently made a name for itself in innovative design – most notably in the ultramodern KKL, Switzerland's fourth-largest museum, which houses a permanent collection of Swiss 19th- and 20th-century art together with temporary avant-garde exhibitions.
KKL Level K, Europaplatz 1. Tel: (041) 226 78 00. www.kunstmuseumluzern.ch. Open: Tue, Thur–Sun 10am–5pm (Wed until 8pm). Admission charge.

Luzern with Mount Rigi in the background

Löwendenkmal (Lion Monument)
The famous 'dying Lion of Luzern'
monument was carved into the cliffs
above town in 1821 in honour of the
heroic Swiss mercenaries killed in
the French Revolution. It was once
described by Mark Twain as 'the
saddest, most moving piece of rock in
the world'.

**Sammlung and Picasso Donation
Rosengart (Rosengart Collection and
Picasso Donation)**
This world-famous gallery shows over
200 works by Paul Cézanne, Paul Klee,
Pablo Picasso, Henri Matisse, Claude
Monet and others owned by local art
dealer Angela Rosengart. In 2008 it
acquired the contents of Luzern's
former Picasso Museum and now
boasts over 130 works by the artist
(including paintings, drawing, ceramics
and sculptures) displayed in five new
rooms, together with an engaging
photographic portrayal of the last

17 years of his life, which he spent on
the French Riviera.
*Pilatussstrasse 10. Tel: (041) 220 16 60.
www.rosengart.ch. Open: Apr–Oct
10am–6pm; Nov–Mar 11am–5pm.
Admission charge.*

**Verkehrshaus der Schweiz
(Swiss Transport Museum)**
The celebrated Swiss Transport
Museum contains every type of
transport imaginable from dugout
canoe to spaceship (including over
60 railway locomotives), chronicling
Switzerland's fascinating history
of transport, telecommunications
and tourism. The Planetarium
simulates space travel, and an
IMAX cinema shows larger-than-
life travel documentaries on a
giant 3-D screen.
*Lidostrasse 5. Tel: (041) 370 44 44.
www.verkehrshaus.ch. Open: Apr–Oct
10am–6pm; Nov–Mar 10am–5pm.
Admission charge.*

Tour: Vierwaldstättersee and Mount Pilatus

The Vierwaldstättersee is known for its breathtaking scenery and the charming traditional villages dotted along its shores, which are easily accessed by nostalgic paddle steamer. Combine this with an ascent of Pilatus, the 'Dragon Mountain', for the very best 360-degree views of Central Switzerland.

Start in Luzern. Allow a full day. See map on p91.

1 Vierwaldstättersee (Lake of the Four Cantons)

The glacial Vierwaldstättersee is one of the most beautiful lakes in Europe, with its finger-like fjords that stretch between steep, forest-clad slopes deep into the mountains. It is a popular area for walking and water sports, including waterskiing, sailing, and swimming in its popular lidos along the shoreline. *Catch a paddle steamer to Weggis or Vitnau.*

2 Weggis and Vitnau

These charming villages are located on the sunny, sheltered, eastern shore of the lake, nestling against the impressive backdrop of Mount Rigi. Often dubbed the 'Innerschweizer Riviera', each village contains attractive buildings adorned with flowers and beautiful lakeside promenades. *Head back to Luzern and change to a different boat to Alpnachstadt, just 15km (9¹/₃ miles) south of Luzern. The journey takes 90 minutes.*

3 Alpnachstadt

The electric cogwheel railway to the top of Mount Pilatus departs from Alpnachstadt. It is the steepest cogwheel railway in the world, running at a 48 per cent gradient. Departures are every 45 minutes (*May–Oct 8.10am–4.50pm*) to the top of Pilatus. *The journey up to the summit of Mount Pilatus takes 30 minutes. Tel: (041) 329 11 11. www.pilatus.ch*

4 Mount Pilatus

It was forbidden to climb Pilatus (2,132m/6,994ft) until the 17th century. According to legend, there was once a dragon that lived there, hence its nickname 'Dragon Mountain'. Then it was thought that the body of Pontius Pilate had been brought here by the devil and locals feared that, if disturbed, his angry ghost would bring about the downfall of Luzern. However, a more likely explanation for this giant, mystic mountain's name comes from the Latin *pileatus*, meaning 'capped', as the summit is often cloud-covered. Two mountain restaurants, two hotels and a large sun terrace await visitors at the top, together with 360-degree views over Luzern and the Alps.

Start your descent in a large cabin-style téléphérique cable car, which travels steeply down over dramatic gorges and cliffs to the village of Fräkmüntegg. Unlike the cogwheel railway, the cable cars operate all year round, take just five minutes, and the last descent is between 4.15pm and 6pm depending on the season.

5 Fräkmüntegg

The longest toboggan run in Europe can be found at Fräkmuntegg, appealing to both young and old with wheeled snow-karts in summer and conventional sledges in winter, descending all the way down to Kriens. There are also restaurants, cafés and a mountain church here, which is used alternately for Catholic and Protestant services.

For a more conventional descent, take the small gondola from Fräkmüntegg, which glides down over dense forests and lush floral meadows to Kriens.

6 Kriens

Sleepy Kriens is popular with families for its superb adventure playground, nature trails, barbecue areas and 100-year-old funicular which climbs the town's own mountain, Sonnenberg. *Catch bus No 1 back to the heart of Luzern.*

Tour: Vierwaldstättersee and Mount Pilatus

Stunning views from the terrace on Mount Pilatus

Traditions

Even in today's modern world, some of Switzerland's oldest traditions live on, especially in remote regions that are proud of their cultural distinctions and unique customs. Many of the celebrations are related to ancient pagan rites, time-honoured Alpine rituals, and the passing of the seasons. Others are just for fun.

Traditional regions

Nowhere is folkloric Switzerland as well preserved as in Appenzellerland, where any celebration is an excuse to don traditional dress – women in stiff-winged tulle caps and lace-edged dresses, and men in yellow breeches, embroidered scarlet waistcoats and a silver earring in their right ear. Traditional crafts and folk music are not so much a tourist attraction as a way of life here, and the Appenzellers are the butt of many Swiss jokes, mocked for their old-fashioned, rustic ways.

The villagers of the Lower Engadine also keep many local customs alive as an expression of their unique Romansh heritage, including Mattinadas (2 January), when children parade through the villages with beautifully decorated sledges, and the popular spring parade of Chalandamarz when children parade with giant cowbells, singing traditional songs. On Easter Sunday in Surselva, the young men of the village gather after dark to fling *trer schibettas* (discs of burning wood) down the valley, while declaring their love for a particular woman – the flight of the disc supposedly predicts the success of the love match.

The Appenzellerland Alpauffahrt

Alpauffahrt and Alpabfahrt

One of the most time-honoured traditions in Alpine regions is the

Alpauffahrt in springtime, when cows are clad in flower garlands, embroidered bridles and giant ornamental bells. They are then processed through the village and onto the summer Alpine pastures by herders in traditional costume. In parts of Valais, a series of cow fights takes place to choose the 'queen of the herd'. It is an ancient, bloodless 'sport', and determines which cow leads the mountain procession. In the autumn, the cattle are returned to the villages in equally flamboyant Alpabfahrt processions.

Children in traditional costume

Steinstossen, Hornussen and Schwingen

As a sports-loving nation, is it hardly surprising that the Swiss have invented some games of their own. *Schwingen*, for instance, is an Alpine version of sumo wrestling, often in traditional dress, while *Steinstossen* involves flinging massive rocks as far as possible. In *Hornussen* tournaments, one person hits a *Hornuss* (a disc) into the air, while another player tries to hit it with a large wooden bat. Look out also for *Waffenlaufen*, when runners dressed in military uniform carry a rifle over courses up to 42km (26 miles) long. Riederalp even has its own Chüfladefäscht (Cow-pat Throwing Festival). On a more domestic level, the Swiss enjoy their national card game of *Jass*.

Gogwärgini and Tschäggättä

In Valais, it is believed that *Gogwärgini* (wild gnomes) used to live in the Fieschertal, helping villagers with their daily chores. Tales of these tiny, bearded folk still live on in the valley, and there's even a special Gogwärginiweg (Gnome Trail) here in their memory. In the nearby Lötschental in February, residents dress up as *Tschäggättä* – hairy monsters with scary wooden masks and gloves dipped in soot that chase after unsuspecting passers-by – just one of numerous annual festivities throughout Switzerland to ward off evil spirits and the vestiges of winter.

Einsiedeln

For over 1,000 years, Einsiedeln has been Switzerland's most important pilgrimage site. Einsiedeln, derived from the word meaning 'hermit' was named after the hermit St Meginrat who withdrew to the wild forest here around AD 828. Following his death, his devotees formed a Benedictine community centred on his self-built altar. When the Bishop of Konstanz came to consecrate the new church in 934, a heavenly voice declared that God Himself had already consecrated the building. The Pope declared this a miracle and devout believers have descended on this small village in the hills of northern Schwyz ever since.

The Titlis cable car

Einsiedeln still has a monastic community of around 100 priests and brothers. The plain sandstone façade of the massive twin-towered abbey belies an extravagant late baroque interior, designed by one of the monks, lavish with colour, gilt and frescoes. The focal point is the black marble Chapel of Our Lady, built over the remains of Meginrat's cell, which contains the celebrated Black Madonna – a wooden statuette of Mary with baby Jesus, blackened by years of candle smoke.

Engelberg and Titlis

Engelberg is Central Switzerland's best-known ski resort, thanks to the presence of the magnificent snowbound Mount Titlis (*www.titlis.ch*), with its distinctive wave-like summit. Year round, this traditional resort draws skiers, snowboarders and freeriders to the Titlis glacier, 2km (1¼ miles) above the village, while thrill-seekers thrive on paragliding, glacier-crevasse abseiling and bungee jumping from a cable car at the top of the mountain (*May–Oct*). Non-skiers enjoy Mount Titlis too, as it offers the highest viewpoint in Central Switzerland (3,238m/10,623ft), restaurants, a sun terrace, an 'ice cave' and a glacier trail, all reached by the world's first revolving cable car.

Engelberg also attracts visitors on day trips to visit its huge Benedictine monastery. The entire valley was once separate from the Swiss Confederation, and governed by the church. Today the monastery can be visited

BOLLYWOOD IN THE ALPS

Engelberg is better known in India than it is in Europe. Recently it has become a popular location for Bollywood movies requiring Alpine scenery. As a direct result, India has become one of Swiss tourism's biggest growth markets, as thousands of fans flock here each summer to visit their favourite Alpine film locations.

together with its Show Cheese Dairy. *Engelberg-Titlis Tourismus, Klosterstrasse 3. Tel: (041) 639 77 77. www.engelberg.ch*

Mount Rigi

Known locally as the 'Island Mountain' as it appears to be surrounded by the waters of lakes Luzern, Zug and Lauerz, the panorama from the top of Mount Rigi is one of Switzerland's most

Rigi's cogwheel train

popular. Many writers have eulogised the mountain: Victor Hugo was enchanted by its beauty during his 19th-century grand tour, and Mark Twain wrote that 'the glimpses from under the curtaining boughs, of blue water, and tiny sailing boats, and beetling cliffs, were as charming as glimpses of dreamland'. Follow in their footsteps by taking Europe's oldest cogwheel train from Vitznau to Rigi-Kulm, from where it is a 200m (656ft) stroll to the summit. There are hiking trails all over the mountain, including several easy routes part-way down to Rigi Kaltbad, where you can either pick up the cogwheel train or return by cable car to Weggis.

Schwyz

The small, gracious town of Schwyz seems an unlikely location for the most important document in Swiss history, but the original Charter of Confederation, signed and sealed on the Rütli meadow on 1 August 1291 is kept here in the Bundesbriefmuseum (Museum of Federal Charters; *Bahnhofstrasse 20. Tel: (041) 819 20 64. Open: Nov–Apr Tue–Fri 9–11.30am & 1.30–5pm, Sat–Sun 1.30–5pm (May–Oct daily 9am–5pm). Admission charge).* Records of the canton of Schwyz date back to AD 972, but it was following a famous victory against the Habsburgs at nearby Morgarten in 1315 that the three neighbouring Schwyz, Uri and Nidwalden cantons became collectively dubbed 'Schwyzers',

Scenic areas surround the St Gotthard Pass

and the whole country became known as Schwyz instead of Helvetia. The façade of the Rathaus (Town Hall) in the main square was painted in 1891 with scenes from Morgarten to commemorate
600 years of confederation.
Schwyz Tourismus, Bahnhofstrasse 4.
Tel: (041) 810 19 91.
www.schwyz-tourismus.ch

St Gotthard Pass

The St Gotthard Pass is a high mountain pass linking the northern, German-speaking part of Switzerland with the Italian-speaking part. For centuries, the pass was rarely used because it was so treacherous. Nowadays, three daily buses (in summer) scale the heights of this wild,

rugged landscape between Andermatt in Uri canton and Airolo in Ticino. At the top, the Museo Nazionale del San Gottardo (St Gotthard Museum; *Open: June–Oct*) chronicles the fascinating history of the pass and the tunnels.

In 1882, the 15km (9^{1}/$_{3}$-mile) St Gotthard Tunnel opened for rail traffic, and in 1980 a 17km (10^{1}/$_{2}$-mile) road tunnel opened, linking Andermatt and Airolo. Now a second rail tunnel (the Gotthard Base Tunnel) is under construction which, when completed in 2018, will be the longest rail tunnel in the world at 57km (35 miles).

Zug

Zug has the lowest tax rates in the country (about half the national average). As a result, it is the richest

SWISS ARMY KNIVES

Schwyz is home to the Swiss army knife, invented in 1884 by young local Karl Elsener who spotted a gap in the market for dependable pocket knives. His factory at Ibach (just south of Schwyz) was originally named after his mother Victoria but, when stainless steel was invented in 1921 and given the designation 'INOX', the factory was rebranded as Victorinox.

place in Switzerland. The affluent, modern town centre, with smart shopping streets, chic street cafés and modern office blocks, is a stark contrast to the compact Old Town, with its pretty cobbled lanes of medieval churches and gabled, frescoed houses, on the banks of the Zugersee (Lake Zug). The lakeside promenades offer spectacular views of Rigi and Pilatus,

and you can tour the lake by boat. The distinctive Zytturm (Clock Tower), with its distinctive blue-and-white-striped roof, is the tallest building here, built as a watchtower in the mid-13th century. Beneath the clock face, shields represent the eight cantons already in the Confederation when the tower was built – Zurich, Bern, Luzern, Uri, Schwyz, Unterwalden, Glarus and Zug.

Zug is also famous for its cherries; the local tipple kirsch (cherry brandy) and the speciality *Zuger Kirschtorte* (a delicious almond cake infused with kirsch) can be tasted throughout the town.

Zug Tourismus, Reisezentrum Zug, Bahnhofplatz. Tel: (041) 723 68 00. www.zug-tourismus.ch

The picture-postcard town of Zug

Eastern Switzerland

Graubünden is the largest and easternmost canton of Switzerland, bordering Liechtenstein, Austria and Italy. It has been important since Roman times for its high Alpine trade routes, including the Maloja and Bernina passes linking north and south Europe. Today, with their mighty mountains and remarkable glaciers, these passes offer some of the world's most scenic train journeys, including the Bernina Express *route and the world-famous* Glacier Express *train.*

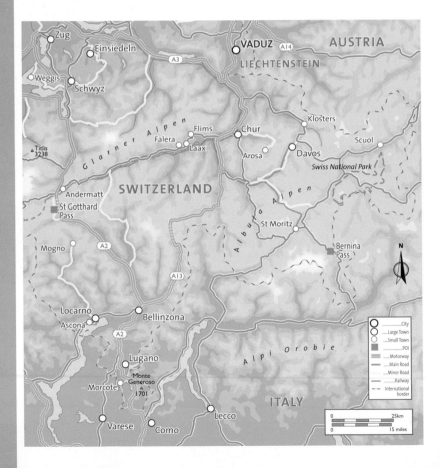

The Corviglia railway runs down into St Moritz

The canton is almost entirely mountainous, and comprises the Swiss National Park (*see p118*), the highlands of the Rhine and Inn river valleys and some of the deepest, most remote valley settlements in Europe – first settled by the Rhaetians, people of Celtic origin. The entire canton has a population of less than 200,000, making an average of just 25 inhabitants per sq km (per ¹/₃ sq mile). Tourism is vital for the region, yet the area remains a wild, beautiful and isolated corner of Switzerland, offering a wide range of holiday resorts from the glamorous winter playgrounds of St Moritz, the world's oldest ski resort, and 'royal' Klosters (the preferred resort of the British royal family), through to quiet mountain villages like Filisur, Scuol and Zuoz.

Some of the finest scenery of the region lies in the Engadine, with its magnificent Silvretta mountains and the Engadine Dolomites. *Engadina* means the 'Valley of the River Inn', which has its source high in the Maloja mountains. The Lower Engadine stretches from Zernez to Martina near the Austrian border. The Upper Engadine extends from Zernez eastwards past St Moritz to Maloja. At its heart, the Swiss National Park is the largest protected area of the country, with some remarkable landscapes and an abundance of flora and fauna.

Eastern Switzerland

GRAUBÜNDEN
Arosa

Over the years, Arosa has developed from an isolated hamlet into one of Graubünden's premier resorts, but without the price tag or pretensions of Klosters or St Moritz. It occupies a broad, sunny, sheltered bowl at the top of the glorious Schanfigg Valley at 1,800m (5,905ft) and, although just 32km (20 miles) southeast of Chur (*see p110*), it remains one of eastern Switzerland's most remote resorts, due to its tortuous approach road, which contains 240 switchbacks.

In winter, Arosa offers small-scale but high-quality skiing suiting all abilities, together with cross-country skiing, ice-skating, curling and tobogganing. In summer, the resort's two lakes provide a focal point for water sports, together with hiking and

Rock climbing in the Engadine

mountain biking and some of the best horse riding in the region.
Arosa Tourismus. Poststrasse. Tel: (081) 378 70 20. www.arosa.ch

Davos and Klosters

As the venue of the annual World Economic Forum and other international congresses, cosmopolitan Davos is often dubbed the 'Global Village', and it is situated on a spectacular lake and surrounded by beautiful mountain peaks. It is a lively, stylish town, with chic shops, sophisticated restaurants, popular walking trails, a buzzing nightlife and a varied programme of cultural events during the summer, including exhibitions at the Kirchner Museum (*Tel: (081) 410 63 00. www.kirchnermuseum.ch. Open: Oct–Nov 2–6pm; Dec–Mar 10am–6pm. Closed Mon*), which contains the world's largest collection of works by local Expressionist artist Ernst Ludwig Kirchner.

However, it is during winter that Davos thrives as one of the nation's top winter sports resorts, with an excellent snow record and Europe's largest natural ice rink. Combined with neighbouring Klosters – famous for its royal British connections with the Prince of Wales – and lesser-known, family-friendly Madrisa, Davos offers over 300km (186 miles) of runs to suit all levels. The Parsenn ski area goes as high as 2,844m (9,330ft), and from there you can ski 12km (7½ miles)

Snowboarding competition in Laax

down to Küblis, with a drop of 2,000m (6,561ft). A free bus service links the different ski areas.

Davos Tourismus, Promenade 67. Tel: (081) 415 21 21. www.davos.ch Klosters Tourismus, Alte Bahnhofstrasse 6. Tel: (081) 410 20 20. www.klosters.ch

Flims, Laax and Falera

The picturesque villages of Flims, Laax and Falera, 20km (12½ miles) west of Chur, together form the extensive Alpenarena ski area, with 220km (137 miles) of pistes for all levels, especially good for intermediate skiers. There are excellent snowboarding areas in Laax, and plenty of avalanche-safe off-piste areas too. During summer months, the area is fantastic for hiking. Two popular trails include the Naturlehrpfad (a circular nature trail near the Cassons summit), and the brief walk to Lag da Cauma near Flims, to row and swim in the lake.

Tourismus Flims, Laax and Falera. Via Nova 62. Tel: (081) 920 92 00. www.alpenarena.ch

HEIDI

The story of Heidi has captured the imagination of generations of readers, film-goers and television audiences worldwide since her author, Johanna Spyri, penned the first story in 1899. The books about the brave heroine from the mountains of Graubünden were set in the countryside around the attractive wine town of Maienfeld, and die-hard fans can walk the Heidiweg (Heidi Footpath) into the Heidialp (Heidi Mountains), or visit the Heidihaus (Heidi's House; *Open: mid-Mar–mid-Nov 10am–5pm. Admission charge*) in the Heididorf (*www.heididorf.ch*), where there is even a shop selling kitsch Heidi memorabilia – children love it!

Skiing and snowboarding

Switzerland is one of the world's best winter sports destinations. After all, this is where winter sports holidays started nearly 150 years ago, when intrepid Alpine skiers had to climb the heights in order to ski down. Swiss ski resorts today have some of the world's best mountain railways, ski lifts and ski schools. Combine this with unspoiled village resorts, huge interconnected ski regions and some of the most spectacular mountain scenery in the Alps, and it is little wonder that Switzerland leads the world in winter sports.

History

It was British aristocrats who invented winter holidays, visiting St Moritz in 1864. Today, it still calls itself the 'Top of the World', and ranks as one of the all-time top resorts, with sensational skiing, plenty of cachet and exclusive palace-hotels imbued with old-world charm. The first ever ski tour of the Alps took place in 1894, from Davos to Arosa, and included Sir Arthur Conan Doyle, author of the Sherlock Holmes novels. The first ski school was organised in 1902 by the Swiss Alpine Club, and one year later the

Skiers take advantage of the fresh powder near Jungfrau

world's first packaged ski holiday took place in Adelboden, organised by Sir Henry Lunn (Lunn's company would eventually become one of the largest travel agents in Britain, Lunn Poly).

While Henry concentrated on developing holidays, his son, Arnold Lunn, took the sport to new heights. He founded the Alpine Ski Club in 1908. In 1921, he organised the first ever downhill ski race (the British National Ski Championships) at Wengen, and in 1922 he invented the slalom in Mürren. Around this time, various devices including rope tows and chairlifts were being introduced in some mountain areas, enabling skiers to complete four or five runs a day. In 1924, Lunn founded the

Skiers and snowboarders side by side on the slopes

Kandahar Ski Club in Mürren, named after a distinguished British Field Marshal. The club still exists today, and organises the notorious annual Inferno Race – the longest downhill race in the world. Finally, in 1931 and 1935, Lunn organised the first World Championships in downhill and slalom racing at Mürren.

In the 1960s, Switzerland managed to avoid most of the ugly resort construction that affected some parts of the Alps. Many of its resorts are small, former farming villages with plenty of character. The main ski regions are in the Bernese Oberland, Graubünden and Valais, and the season stretches from mid-December to mid-April (with year-round glacier skiing in some resorts). Ski schools start lessons for children aged as young as three, and many resorts provide free ski passes for children.

SKIING VS SNOWBOARDING

Most skiers in Switzerland prefer downhill (alpine) skiing, although cross-country skiing is popular too, with 5,000km (3,107 miles) of marked trails, especially in the Engadine and the Jura. You may occasionally see a *velogemel* (snowbike), or a mono-ski – a single, extra-wide ski into which both feet are strapped side by side. The snowboard is a cross between the mono-ski and the surfboard, and is now such a popular sport that resorts have to construct increasingly elaborate freestyle parks to keep up with skill and demand. Look out on the pistes for the different types of snowboarder: freestylers (the acrobats), carvers (the speed freaks) and freeriders, who seek out the ungroomed terrain.

THE ENGADINE
Scuol

Together with neighbouring villages Zuoz and Guarda, this beautiful settlement is a showcase of Engadine architecture. Its ancient, distinctive houses have thick walls decorated with traditional sgraffito designs, small windows, and arched, carved, wooden doorways.

The area is rich in history. First settled by the Rhaetians during the Bronze Age, it later became the Roman province of Rhaetia and was eventually split into the Lower Engadine and the Upper Engadine by Charlemagne. Scuol's main attraction, however, is the modern Bogn Engiadina spa complex, with its range of hot and cold pools, saunas, massage jets and Roman baths. Above the resort, there is skiing, with

RHAETO-ROMANSH

Rhaeto-Romansh is Switzerland's fourth language (after French, German and Italian) and the main language of around 70,000 people in Graubünden. It is most commonly spoken in the Engadine regions of Oberhalfstein and the Bündner Oberland. Derived from Latin, the language has survived over the centuries due to the isolation of these remote mountain communities. In 1938, an amendment to the Swiss Constitution confirmed it as a national language, and in 1996 it was elevated to the status of 'semi-official language'. Although only spoken by less than one per cent of the population, the Romansh people are immensely proud of their culture, preserving it through literature, poetry and even two Romansh radio stations.

80km (50 miles) of well-groomed runs up to a height of 2,800m (9,186ft). *Tourismus Scuol. Tel: (081) 861 22 22. www.scuol.ch*

The centre of Guarda village

The *Bernina Express* traverses the Bernina Pass

St Moritz

With more 4- and 5-star hotel rooms than anywhere else in Europe, sensational mountain cuisine, deluxe designer boutiques and a lakeside setting in one of Switzerland's most beautiful valleys, St Moritz hardly needs skiing. The town itself is surprisingly ugly, yet it is the oldest winter resort in the world, drawing visitors to its slopes since 1894. For this is the winter playground of the rich and famous – with 350km (217 miles) of superb, sunny 'see-and-be-seen' slopes – where fashions are formed and new trends launched.

As the cradle of winter sports, it seems only appropriate that St Moritz offers such unique Alpine spectacles as polo and horse racing on ice, snow cricket and snow golf – all set on the spectacular frozen lake. However, it is the Olympic Bob Run and the Cresta Run's 145kph (90mph) sledge track (at nearby Celerina) that still offer the most exciting ice events in the world.

Kur- und Verkehrsverein St Moritz, via Maistra 12. Tel: (081) 837 33 33.
www.stmoritz.ch

Bernina Pass

The *Bernina Express* is a must for every visitor to Graubünden – one of the world's most beautiful railway routes, from Chur via St Moritz to Tirano in Italy. The journey, over the Bernina Pass (2,253m/7,391ft), is the only north–south rail crossing in the Alps, and journeys through varying cultures and regions, with striking geographical contrasts from the snowy summits and mighty glaciers of the Bernina Pass to the Renaissance *palazzi* and palm trees of Tirano. Highlights include the curved Landwasser Viaduct (*see p110*), the unique circular viaduct at Brusio, and countless loop tunnels and horseshoe bends.
Bernina Express, Rhätische Bahn, Bahnhofstrasse 25, Chur.
Tel: (081) 288 61 00.
www.rhb.ch

Train ride: *Glacier Express*

Book early for a ride on the self-confessed 'slowest express train in the world' from St Moritz to Zermatt (or vice versa) – a remarkable eight-hour railway journey over 291 bridges, through 91 tunnels and over the spectacular Oberalp Pass at the very heart of Switzerland (www.glacierexpress.ch).

St Moritz/Davos

Start your journey on the Rhaetian railway at the glamorous ski resort of St Moritz, lovingly dubbed the 'Top of the World'.

The train passes through the 5.8km (3½-mile) Albula Tunnel, then loops and zigzags up the Albula line, rising more than 400m (1,312ft) in just 5km (3 miles) en route to Filisur.

Landwasser Viaduct

Just after Filisur, the train enters a tunnel and emerges atop the Landwasser Viaduct, high above the wild, rocky Landwasser gorge. This massive curving viaduct is the longest bridge on the Rhätische Bahn's network at 285m (935ft).

The train proceeds down to Chur, past fortresses and castles.

Chur

Chur is one of Switzerland's oldest cities, inhabited since Roman times, and the capital of Graubünden. It is set in a deep valley, carved by the River Rhine, at the lowest point of the train trip (just under 600m/1,968ft). The medieval cobbled streets of the Old Town are dominated by a huge 12th-century cathedral.

The train follows the Rhine gorge, sometimes called the 'Grand Canyon of Switzerland' for its dramatic scenery, past the 17th-century Reichenau Castle and up to Disentis.

Disentis and the Oberalp Pass

A massive 8th-century Benedictine monastery with distinctive baroque twin towers dominates Disentis. The Matterhorn Gotthard Bahn railway, with its cogwheel mechanisms, takes over here and the train slowly climbs up the Oberalp Pass, past breathtaking vistas of vast, glistening-white mountains, to the highest point of the journey (the Oberalp Passhöhe) at 2,033m (6,670ft).

A hair-raisingly steep, winding descent takes you to Andermatt.

Andermatt

This small town at the crossroads of the Swiss Alps, surrounded by peaks, has been crossed for centuries by merchants and travellers, but is today best known for its exceptional skiing and hiking.

The descent from Andermatt to Brig is more gradual. Just after Andermatt, the train passes through the Furka Tunnel for 20 minutes. It re-emerges into the German-speaking part of Valais and the Upper Rhône Valley. On the right are glimpses of the Aletsch Gletscher (see p82).

Brig

This important German-speaking, historic valley town is of strategic geographical importance. Close to the border, with strong Italianate influences, it is the nerve centre of the region, and a gateway to the north (to Bern), the south (to Italy), the west (to Geneva) and to the high Alpine passes of the northeast. The Stockalperschloss (Stockalper Castle) here, with its eccentric onion domes, was funded with trade profits from the Simplon Pass by local merchant Kaspar Jodok von Stockalper in the 17th century.

The final stretch of the train journey is a steep ascent up the beautiful Mattertal (Matter Valley) to Zermatt, which commences after the town of Visp in the Rhône Valley.

Zermatt

Fittingly, this epic rail journey ends in one of the world's most famous resorts, situated just in front of the majestic 4,478m (14,691ft) high Matterhorn – Switzerland's landmark mountain.

Glorious views from the *Glacier Express*

Ticino

Ticino is the southern, Italian-speaking tip of Switzerland, and the nation's fourth-largest canton. It is a balmy region of medieval castles, baroque palazzi, and quaint villages, where pizza, polenta and pasta are served on sun-kissed piazzas, and where the mild Mediterranean climate encourages the lush vegetation and subtropical gardens famous throughout Switzerland.

See map on p102.

The name of the canton is taken from the River Ticino, a tributary of northern Italy's River Po, and the canton's proximity to Italy is reflected in the architecture and cuisine. Many buildings are made of stone, with slate or terracotta tiled roofs resembling those of Lombardy or Tuscany.

The lakeside resorts combine Swiss efficiency with a distinctly Italianate atmosphere, thanks to the laid-back, light-hearted disposition of the locals, the pastel-coloured houses in ice cream shades, and the popular pavement café culture. However, relations between Switzerland and Italy were not always as peaceful. Ticino was carved out of the Duchy of Milan by Swiss soldiers in the late 15th century following centuries of bloody battles.

Getting to Ticino is always an adventure. One of the most dramatic routes is over the Simplon Pass, from German-speaking Brig, and down to the Italian border town of Domodossola, or by train through the

Simplon Tunnel – at 20km (12 miles), one of the longest railway tunnels in the world. For centuries, travellers crossed the St Gotthard Pass – a major Alpine route from north to south. However, nowadays, people usually opt to go through the tunnel (*see p99*).

Chiesa di San Giovanni Battista, Mogno

Alfresco dining beside Lake Maggiore in Ascona

Alternatively, the *Bernina Express* (*see p109*) takes four scenic hours from Chur to Tirano, followed by a bus ride to Lugano.

Most visitors to Ticino head straight to its southern resorts – Lugano, Locarno and Ascona – which share the warm waters of glittering lakes Lugano and Maggiore with Italy. Over the centuries, the beautiful old towns of Locarno and Ascona with their attractive lakeside locations have drawn writers, painters and scholars to the shores of Lake Maggiore, including Lenin, Carl Jung, Rudolf Steiner, Hermann Hesse and Paul Klee. Lake cruises are a gentle and popular way to admire the local scenery and to explore southern Ticino's fishing villages and waterside gardens.

It is also worth spending time exploring the wild Alpine valleys of northern Ticino – areas of towering mountains, dark forests and fast-flowing streams, with unspoiled villages and proud locals. The canton is rich in footpaths and trekking trails, many of which are accessed by cable cars and mountain railways. Monte San Salvatore and Monte Generoso offer some of the best aerial views of the region.

Ticino Tourism, via Lugano 12. Tel: (091) 825 70 56. www.ticino.ch

Ascona

Once a tiny fishing port, stylish Ascona is now a flourishing resort that rivals its larger neighbour, Locarno, across the Maggia river delta. Its main attractions are the Museum of Modern Art, a lovely lakeside promenade and large beach, a golf course, great shopping, and a handful of popular restaurants.
Turismo Ascona, via Papio 5. Tel: (091) 791 00 91. www.ascona.ch

Bellinzona

The capital of Ticino is an impressive city, dominated by its three medieval fortifications, the Tre Castelli (Three Castles). Built by the Dukes of Milan to protect the city from the bellicose Swiss, the castles illustrate Bellinzona's strategic importance as the gateway to Italy from the north, and the Alps from the south, and they are listed as a UNESCO World Cultural Heritage Site. The largest, Castelgrande (*www.castelgrande.ch*), is easily accessed by lift from Piazza del Sole. It has an archaeological museum, restaurant, and magnificent views across the Magadino plain. Castello di Montebello (*www.castellodimontebello. com*) is the most picturesque, and Castello di Sasso Corbaro (*www.sasso-corbaro.ch*) hosts temporary art exhibitions. In the city centre, the old town contains some magnificent town houses, several typically Ticinese taverns (known as *grottos* or *canvetti*) and the Villa dei Cedri (*www.villacedri.ch*), set in a beautiful park of cedar trees where the Museum of Modern Art contains works by artists from Switzerland and Lombardy.
Bellinzona Turismo, Palazzo Civico. Tel: (091) 825 21 31. www.bellinzonaturismo.ch

Mountain bikers visiting Castelgrande in Bellinzona

Locarno

The popular resort of Locarno, on the northernmost shore of Lake Maggiore, boasts Switzerland's mildest climate. It is a beautiful old town surrounded by vine-clad hillsides. The area once belonged to Lombardy and the town's 14th-century castle, formerly owned by the wealthy Milanese Visconti family, is a reminder of former times. A small electric train tours the Città Vecchia (Old Town) with its sun-drenched plazas framed by fine patrician houses, elegant arcades of galleries, shops and restaurants, and beautiful churches – all centred round Piazza Grande, with its popular pavement cafés.

Locarno's extensive art collections are housed in a beautiful 18th-century palace, the Pinacoteca Casa Rusca, and contain an important group of works by Jean Arp and other celebrated Dadaists. The lakeside park of Giardini Jean Arp also has some fascinating sculptures by the Alsatian surrealist artist, who is buried in the cemetery here.

The lakeside promenade is fringed with palm trees and the beach lido is among Switzerland's best. From here, boats tour the villages and resorts of the lake including Isole de Brissago, a botanical island that has a collection of rare plants and flowers from all over the world. Above the town, the Cardada hills offer impressive views and fantastic walking opportunities with easy access by cable car.

Hiking in the hills above Locarno and Lake Maggiore

Ente Turistico Lago Maggiore, via B Luini 3. Tel: (091) 791 00 91. www.maggiore.ch

Santuario della Madonna del Sasso (Church of Madonna del Sasso)

The Church of Madonna del Sasso, the patron saint of Locarno, is located high above the town with magnificent views over the lake and mountains beyond. It is the most famous church of pilgrimage in Italian-speaking Switzerland, easily accessed on foot (allow 20 minutes) or by funicular from the town centre.

Via del Santuario. Tel: (091) 743 62 65. Open: 2–5pm. Admission charge.

Typical arcaded architecture in Lugano

Lugano

Ticino's largest town is situated in a picturesque bay on the shores of Lake Lugano, between Monte Brè and the impressive Monte San Salvatore. With its luxuriant vegetation, palm-lined promenades and glittering azure lake, it oozes Mediterranean flair. Its ancient centre is car-free and typically Italianate in style, with narrow twisting streets of pastel-coloured houses, arcades and sun-bleached squares. Above the terracotta-tiled rooftops rises the Cathedral of St Lawrence, its façade considered to be one of Ticino's most impressive early Renaissance works.

Lugano is Switzerland's third most important financial centre, full of banks and businesses, and its prices are correspondingly high. Shopping is chic, with boutiques featuring the latest fashions from Milan and an abundance of exquisite chocolate shops. There is even chocolate tasting here (*see p77*). It is also the home town of leading Swiss architect Mario Botta. His works punctuate the city, distinguished by their simple, geometrical lines, and include the casino, the bus terminal, which has a canopy that changes colour with the seasons, and the Banca del Gottardo, which also contains a gallery and restaurant.

Lake Lugano is popular for water sports, especially sailing, waterskiing and windsurfing. For a bird's-eye view of the resort, take the funicular from Paradiso up to the viewpoint atop Monte San Salvatore, where there is also a botanical park containing rare wild flowers.

Lugano Turismo, Palazzo Civico-Riva Albertolli. Tel: (091) 913 32 32. www.lugano-tourism.ch

Mogno

The main reason to visit this off-the-beaten-track hamlet, 60km (37 miles) north of Locarno, is the striking Chiesa di San Giovanni Battista (Chapel of St John the Baptist) designed by local architect Mario Botta (*see p56*). The original chapel was destroyed in an avalanche in 1986. Ten years later, Botta created a veritable masterpiece of futuristic sacred architecture in striped grey granite and white marble (from Peccia in Val Maggia) with a glass roof, as a gift to the village.

Monte Generoso

The summit of Monte Generoso (1,701m/5,580ft), on the Italo–Swiss border, offers the finest views in Ticino. It is best approached from Lugano by boat to Capolago, followed by a 40-minute cogwheel train ride through wild countryside to the mountain station at the top. From here, on a clear day, you can see lakes Como, Lugano and Maggiore, the Alps and the Apennines.

Ferrovia Monte Generoso. Tel: (091) 630 51 11. www.montegeneroso.ch

Morcote

Tumbling down the lower slopes of Monte Abostora on the shores of Lake Lugano, the former fishing village of Morcote is one of the most picture-perfect villages in Ticino, easily accessed by boat from Lugano. Atop the village, the ancient Chiesa di Madonna del Sasso (Chapel of Madonna del Sasso), with its impressive bell tower, contains some beautiful 16th-century frescoes. From the church, more than 400 steps lead down through a maze of alleyways, lanes and arcaded patrician houses to the lakeshore and the unusual Parco Scherrer (Scherrer Park), rich with subtropical flora and an eclectic collection of architectural features and sculpture. 1km (²/₃ mile) north of Morcote, the smaller village of Vico Morcote is equally pretty but less touristic.

Turismo Morcote. Tel: (091) 996 11 20. www.promorcote.ch

Pretty Morcote beside Lake Lugano

Ticino

Getting away from it all

Despite Switzerland's comparatively small size and its vast number of visitors (over 120 million a year), there are still some hidden corners waiting to be discovered, away from the well-trodden tourist track. What's more, you don't need to be clinging to a mountain peak or even on a high Alpine pass in order to see them.

Schweizerischer Nationalpark (Swiss National Park)

The Swiss National Park is Switzerland's only national park and the largest protected area in the country. It is located in the canton of Graubünden in eastern Switzerland, and occupies 169sq km (65 sq miles) of magnificent Alpine countryside adjoining the Italian border 24km (15 miles) northeast of St Moritz. The

There are hiking trails all over the park

park was established in 1914, and has been designated a 'category one nature reserve', which provides the highest protection levels for flora and fauna – this means no tree felling, grazing, flower picking, hunting or fishing is permitted, and walkers have to stick to the footpaths. The Ofen Pass or Pass dal Fuorn (2,149m/7,050ft) is the main road through the park, from which hiking trails extend in all directions.

The information centre at Zernez (*Open: June–Oct*) details the park's three main aims – nature conservation, scientific research and environmental education – as well as the park's unique vegetation and wildlife, which includes ibex, chamois, red deer, martens, foxes, marmots, eagles, bearded vultures and other birds. A nature trail near the pass is especially popular with families.

With luck and patience, you can see a wide variety of birds and animals, whatever month you visit. From June to the end of August, the magnificent

Glorious scenery in the Swiss National Park

Alpine flora is in full bloom. In July and August, the last of the snow melts, opening up magnificent high-altitude hiking routes. In late September the valleys echo with the barking of stags during the red deer mating season, and in October the autumnal colours of the trees are spectacular.

Around the Swiss National Park

The train trip from St Moritz to Scuol-Tarasp is particularly scenic, travelling through the wild Engadine Valley, with the Swiss National Park visible for much of the journey. The route starts in the Upper Engadine Valley, which stretches from Zernez to Maloja. This area is one of the driest, sunniest and most picturesque regions, thanks to the beautiful Engadine Dolomites and Silvretta mountains. Wonderful hikes here include Val Roseg (near

Pontresina), Isola and the lake of Sils near Maloja. The scenic Lower Engadine Valley stretches from Zernez to Martina near the Austrian border and contains some of the most quaint and far-flung villages of Switzerland. *Nationalpark Haus Zernez. Tel: (081) 851 41 41. www.nationalpark.ch*

BEARDED VULTURES ON THE MOVE

The bearded vulture, with its amazing 3m (10ft) wingspan, would be extinct in the Alps if not for a remarkable reintroduction programme of baby vultures, released into the Stabelchod Valley in the 1990s, which have since bred successfully. Since June 2005, the park has tracked several young bearded vultures – including Blick and Samuel – using tiny satellite transmitters, as part of the 'Bearded Vultures on the Move' project. Their remarkable journeys can be followed at *www.bartgeier.ch*

The Montfort cable car above Verbier

Although there is only one official national park in Switzerland, the majority of the country resembles a giant nature park. From the valleys of the Mittelland (Middle Land) through to the high Alpine summits, there is an astonishing range of flora and fauna to thrill the most devoted naturalist, and the diversity of birdlife is one of the richest in Europe. At higher altitudes, the most commonly observed wild animals are deer. Ibex, chamois and marmots are less easy to see.

Nature trails

Verbier has a devoted Sentier des Chamois (Chamois Trail), a two-day trek starting at dawn from the Montfort cabin, which is ideal for spotting mountain goats, ibex, marmots and birds of prey. Other nature trails (with helpful information panels along the routes) include the Wolf Trail – a two-hour trek from Eischoll, near Visp, to Ergisch, and the Lynx Trail – a 4km (2½-mile) hike on the Betelberg Mountain near Lenk, where two lynx were caught in 1997 and tagged with transmitters. The Marmot Trail starts at the top station of the Schönbiel cable car at Bettmeralp and ends at the beautiful Bettmer lake. Luckily it is a beautiful walk, as these small, endearing creatures are very elusive. You may have more luck spotting them at Saas Fee early in the morning. Start at Längfluh hut and bring a bag of carrots – you may even get close enough to feed them!

The Saastal offers some exceptional off-the-beaten-track walking, with its massive larch forests surrounded by 4,000m (13,124ft) peaks, its unusually high tree line, and rich, colourful Alpine flora. You may see marmots, chamois and ibex on many different

MOUNTAIN PROTECTION

The Swiss are fanatical about preserving their beautiful countryside and have some of the world's strongest environmental legislation. In 1991, the government implemented the Alpine Convention, seeking to reduce damage caused by motor traffic and tourism. On a more personal level, the Swiss are Europe's leading recyclers. In their beloved mountains, they follow a strict series of unwritten rules. These include never picking Alpine wild flowers, sticking to marked paths when hiking, leaving farm gates as they find them, only lighting fires in permitted locations, and taking all rubbish home with them. They expect visitors to do the same!

hiking paths in the early morning hours, and possibly even a rare golden eagle circling overhead. The Forest Educational Trail from Furggstalden to Saas-Almagell provides a fascinating insight into forest life and its inhabitants, and the Alpine Flower Walk from Kreuzboden to Saas-Grund features 240 different plant species, some of which are only found in the Saas Valley.

One of the nation's prettiest walking destinations is the Oeschinensee, a beautiful, blue glacial lake at the head of the Kander Valley in the Bernese Oberland. This U-shaped valley is famed for its diversity of wildlife, its rare orchids and lilies, cascading waterfalls and dazzling views. Start at Kandersteg, a friendly, traditional village of pretty chalet buildings, and take the Oeschinen lift for the short walk to the blue lake surrounded by jagged peaks of the Blüemlisalp mountain range.

Getting away from it all

The Kander Valley and Oeschinensee

There is no need to be in the high Alps to escape the crowds. The lowlands, the pre-Alps, Ticino and the Jura offer rewarding driving routes, landmark sights and deserted walking trails with magnificent scenery too. Visit the largest underground waterfalls in Europe at the Trümmelbach Falls near Lauterbrunnen, and the spectacular Giessbach Falls nearby, at Brienz.

Country walks and tours

In the pre-Alps near Gruyères, the Vallon des Mortheys is an especially pleasant trail, with its rich flora and fauna and scenery. The little-visited medieval town of Murten, north of Fribourg on the

Giessbach Falls, Brienz

OFF THE BEATEN TRACK

To escape the crowds and to be totally at one with nature, head for the high Alpine hiking paths (*see p80*). These are exclusively for experienced mountain walkers, with mountain guides and all the proper attire. Some mountain guide companies offer multi-day hut-to-hut treks, where the only people you are likely to meet are fellow walkers. For the ultimate in escapism, book into one of Switzerland's highly revered mountaineering schools. Contact the Swiss Mountain Sports School Association for details (*www.bergsportschulen.ch*). Remember, however, that mountaineering is not for the uninitiated, and should never be undertaken alone or without all the necessary paraphernalia. One alternative is to try your hand at *via ferrata* (*www.viaferrata.org*) – specially designed ladders embedded in the rocks, giving hikers a taste of rock climbing with the bare minimum of equipment (helmet, gloves, etc).

shore of beautiful Murtensee (Lake Murten), is well worth exploring. Here too is the Sentier du Vins de Vully (Vully Wine Trail). Canals and cycle paths link the Murtensee with Lac de Neuchâtel (Neuchâtel Lake) and the Bielersee (Lake Biel) to form the Pays des Trois Lacs (Three Lakes Region).

The Jura offers gentle landscapes for touring, and impressive walks up the Gorge de l'Areuse, and to the Saut du Doubs waterfall, and the striking Creux-du-van cirque, each with their remarkable Jurassic rock formations. Appenzellerland is attractive for car tours, with its verdant, rolling hillsides and rustic villages. It also has spectacular walks to Seealp and Ebenalp.

Vines on the shores of Murtensee

In Ticino, three twisting valleys north of Locarno – Val Verzasca, Valle Maggia and Val Bavona – contain some of the canton's most beautiful scenery. With their remote grey-stone villages, tiny churches, ancient bridges, mountain streams and wooded hillsides on the southern slopes of the Alps, they offer fantastic walking and touring opportunities. South of Lago di Lugano, the pyramid-shaped mountain, Monte San Giorgio, safeguards the world's best fossil record of marine life from the Triassic period (245–230 million years ago), and is listed as a UNESCO World Heritage Site.

Spas and thermal springs

Bathing in thermal springs has long been popular in Switzerland, and Leukerbad is the country's largest 'wellness' resort with over 3.9 million litres (858,000 gallons) of thermal water at a temperature of 51°C (123°F) feeding 22 public and private swimming pools daily (*Leukerbad. Tel: (027) 472 71 71. www.leukerbad.ch*). The latest craze is for designer spas as a retreat from urban life. Some of the most popular include Therme Vals, the St Moritz Spa, Bad Scuol, the Bergoase in Arosa and the new Dolder Grand Spa in Zurich (*see p140*).

When to go

Despite its small size, Switzerland has a surprising variety of microclimates. The Atlantic Ocean influences weather in the west, bringing winds, moisture and rainfall, while the climate in the east has generally higher temperatures, more sunshine and less precipitation. South of the Alps in Ticino, the climate is almost Mediterranean, with mild seasons and significantly higher temperatures but, due to the immediate vicinity of the Alps to the north, a large amount of rainfall.

Alpine weather

Much of Switzerland is mountainous. Temperatures are generally lower in the high Alpine regions, while the Mittelland (Middle Land) plateaux and the northern regions have higher temperatures and warmer summers. The elements can change quickly in the Alps, and so it is important to check the local weather forecast before venturing into the mountains, even during summer months.

Seasons

Switzerland has four distinct seasons, each with its different appeal. Spring (March to May) is a lovely time to visit, before the summer crowds. The weather is generally mild, but it can be changeable, rainy and cool. The snow is melting, the rivers and waterfalls are at their most dramatic and the countryside is fresh and green.

Summer (June to August) is usually warm and dry, with average temperatures around 22°C (71°F) in the cities and low-lying valleys, rarely rising above 30°C (86°F), and with pleasant humidity levels. In the cities, this is the season of al fresco dining, of lazy days, long balmy evenings and swimming in the lakes. The weather is slightly cooler in the mountains, depending on the elevation – at the height of summer, the zero line (0°C or 32°F) may rise as high as 4,000m (13,124ft) above sea level. This is a magnificent time for hiking, mountain biking and other outdoor sports, when the meadows are ablaze with Alpine flowers.

Autumn (September to November) is another popular time to visit, with plenty of crisp, clear, sunny days, although it can become quite cool. In the mountains, the zero line drops to around 2,000m (6,560ft) above sea level. The cities are quieter and there are often some excellent bargains in the shops. In the late autumn, the trees in the mountains start to change colour, painting the landscape with a distinctive golden hue. It is also the season of delicious game dishes and hearty stews.

It can be beautiful in winter when the sun shines

Winter (December to February) is supposed to be cold and dry, with plenty of snow in the mountains. The temperature may drop below 0°C (32°F) everywhere in the country, especially at night, and the towns and cities at low elevations may even get a sprinkling of snow periodically. Winter is always a magical time to visit. The towns and villages are elaborately decorated for Christmas with fairy lights illuminating the streets; and the aromas of gingerbread and Glühwein fill the air from numerous Christmas markets. It is also the ski season, drawing crowds of Swiss and foreign visitors to the slopes for some of the best skiing in Europe.

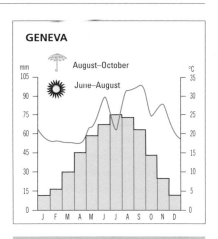

GENEVA

August–October

June–August

WEATHER CONVERSION CHART

25.4mm = 1 inch

°F = 1.8 × °C + 32

Getting around

Public transport in Switzerland is swift, prompt and as dependable as a Swiss watch, making touring the country a real pleasure. Indeed, the public transport system is so good that everyone uses it, leaving little or no need for your own car, unless you hope to visit some of the more far-flung mountainous corners of the nation. Train times are integrated with bus and ferry services, and the Swiss travel system offers some excellent discount passes for visitors.

Swiss travel system

Swiss people rarely pay full fare on their public transport system and you should do the same by opting for one of a number of excellent travel passes.

The Swiss Pass (available for 4, 8, 15 or 22 days or one month) gives unlimited travel on trains, buses and boats, and many city transport networks, as well as reduced-price travel on other private mountain railways and cable cars, and free admission to most museums. The Swiss Flexi Pass, available for 3, 4, 5 or 6 non-consecutive days within one month, gives free travel on those days plus a 50% reduction on train, bus and boat rides on days in between. The Family Card allows children up to 16 years of age free travel when accompanied by a parent. The Swiss Youth Pass is a reduced-rate Swiss Pass for passengers up to 26 years of age. There are also regional tickets for unlimited travel, and a Swiss Transfer Ticket which allows return travel from a Swiss border or airport to a selected destination. All these schemes are in a

booklet available from Switzerland Tourism (*www.myswitzerland.com*).

By rail

The swift, punctual Swiss railway network is among the best in the world, operated by Swiss Federal Railways – the SBB (Schweizerische Bundesbahnen; *www.sbb.ch*). The railways provide easy, stress-free, efficient transportation to all the cantons. Some routes are operated by private companies. Many mountain routes, including the *Glacier Express* train route (*see p110*) and the *Bernina Express* (*see p109*), are an attraction in their own right.

Timetable information for SBB trains is available at any Swiss train station or at *www.rail.ch*. There are dining cars on many trains, and the main routes also have a dedicated family carriage.

By air

The main airports are at Zurich and Geneva, with three secondary airports at Basel, Bern and Lugano (*see p144*). All domestic services are operated by Swiss (*www.swiss.com*). Flights are fast but expensive, and many business people prefer to travel by train or car.

By road

There is little need for a car in Switzerland as the public transport system is so reliable. An efficient bus network connects all the main cities, and *PostBuses* operate on some more remote routes (*www.postbus.ch/travel*).

If you are planning to explore by car, there are several hire car companies at the main airports. If you are bringing your own car, you need to purchase a *vignette* (annual motorway tax, valid for one year) on entering Switzerland. Failure to display one on a motorway can result in a hefty fine. Ensure also that you have the appropriate insurance, and remember your insurance documents and driver's licence.

As a general rule, names of towns are used for navigation on the roads, rather than highway numbers. In the summer and at weekends, roads can become congested, including the Gotthard Tunnel and the Zurich–Bern motorway. In winter, many roads in the mountains are closed; chains or winter tyres may also be necessary.

By taxi

Taxis are generally pricey and can be picked up at ranks. Some cities, including Geneva, Zurich and Luzern, have water taxis during the summer months.

By boat

During the summer, passenger boats ply the major lakes and rivers, many with onboard dining and special excursions. The old paddle steamers on the lakes of Brienz, Geneva, Luzern and Zurich are especially appealing.

City transport networks

The public transport system in most cities is interlinked, which means you only need one ticket, whether you travel by tram, bus, boat or train. Urban networks are divided into zones, and fares are calculated by how many zones you travel in. There is a timetable of zones and services at each stop, together with vending machines. You must buy a ticket before you embark and stamp it in one of the special validation machines at the transport stop. Many cities have trams, and a suburban commuter rail network called the S-Bahn (*Stadtschnellbahn* or 'fast city train'). In 2008 Lausanne became Switzerland's first city (and the smallest city in the world) to have a full metro system.

Ask at the tourist office for details of special passes that offer unlimited travel on urban public transport.

Travellers with disabilities

Switzerland is well prepared to receive travellers with disabilities, and the facilities are generally of a high standard. Mobility International Switzerland (*Tel: (062) 206 88 35. www.mis-ch.ch*) is an excellent source of information.

Accommodation

Switzerland is world famous for its hospitality, and its hotels are among the best in the world, focusing on high levels of service and value for money. Whatever your price range, accommodation is always of a high quality, whether you choose a simple family guesthouse or a palatial spa-hotel.

Hotels

Most hotels are affiliated to the Schweizer Hotelier Verein (Swiss Hotels Association), which classifies all the listings according to a 5-star rating system (from a basic 1 star through to luxury 5 stars). Price rates in cities are fairly constant throughout the year, but in small towns and resorts there are low, middle and high seasons. Some

The Park Hotel in Vitznau, Luzern

mountain resorts have two high seasons – one in summer, and one in winter for skiing. Local tourist offices have listings and are usually happy to book a hotel for you. A service charge of 15 per cent is included in hotel bills, and an additional local tax may be payable depending on the location.

Budget options

There is a wide choice of budget accommodation, ranging from camping to youth hostels and simple B&Bs.

Camping

Like the hotels, most of the nation's 450 campsites are classified from 1 to 5 stars depending on their amenities. Many are in out-of-the-way, scenic locations best reached by car, although some are easily accessible by public transport. Camping guides published by the TCS (Swiss Touring Club, *www.tcs.ch*) can be purchased from Switzerland Tourism (*www.myswitzerland.com*). Camping rough is against the law. For the ultimate in rooms with a view, keen walkers should consider staying in a mountain hut on the top of a mountain.

Accommodation

B&Bs

There are over 350 B&Bs throughout the country, listed at *www.bnb.ch*. Look out also for signs outside private homes advertising *Zimmer frei*, *chambres libres* or *camere libere* ('rooms available' in German, French or Italian).

Self-catering

Self-catering accommodation is usually booked months in advance, especially in ski resorts or popular summer vacation destinations. In the mountains, rustic mountain inns (*Berghaus*, *auberge de montagne*) are good for affordable accommodation with lots of character.

Youth hostels

Another top budget option is a youth hostel or a 'backpacker'. Swiss hostels tend to be of a higher standard than your average youth hostel, and are extremely popular with families. They have clean, comfortable dormitories and often a choice of double and family rooms. Book well in advance, especially in cities during the summer months and in ski resorts during winter. There are two main hostelling associations in Switzerland: Swiss Youth Hostels (*www.youthhostel.ch*), affiliated to the Hostelling International network, and a small group of independent

Sleep like an Eskimo in an igloo village

hostels, called Swiss Backpackers (*www.backpacker.ch*). A list of hostels is obtainable from Switzerland Tourism (*www.myswitzerland.com*).

Unusual accommodation

When the cows are on the Alpine pastures in summer, some Swiss farmers have collaborated to offer a 'Sleeping in the Straw' programme (Schlaf im Stroh, Aventure sur la Paille; *www.abenteuer-stroh.ch*) – charging tourists a nominal rate to sleep in their empty barns. Children love it, but don't forget to bring your sleeping bag! For the ultimate, Alpine chill-out, spend the night in an igloo. There are currently four igloo villages (*www.iglu-dorf.com*) in Switzerland – in Davos-Klosters, Engelberg, Gstaad and Zermatt. Choose from 'standard' multi-bed igloos for families or a variety of 'romantic igloo' packages, including saunas, fondues and Glühwein (*see p170*).

Food and drink

Swiss cuisine combines the very best culinary characteristics of France, Italy and Germany with simple, nourishing local dishes that have developed over the centuries in the valleys and mountain regions. Each canton has its own traditional and regional specialities and, in recent years, innovative vintners and talented young chefs have put Switzerland on the map as a culinary centre.

The nation's culinary identity is closely linked with its geographical characteristics. Its predominantly mountainous terrain has given rise to simple, yet rich and substantial *cuisine du terroir* (country cooking). The Alpine streams and lakes provide an abundant variety of fresh fish, and the lush mountain pastures produce the creamiest milk, butter and cream – and cheeses that are the envy of the world.

Cheese dishes reign supreme in Swiss fare, with delicious, runny *raclettes* and fondues (*see p49*) commonplace on menus nationwide. Fondues can also be meat-based, dipped into hot oil (*fondue bourguignonne*) or into mulled wine (*fondue Bacchus*). Soups are popular too – often a meal in themselves – ranging from chalet soup (made with cream, cheese, vegetables and pasta) to the chunky vegetable Bern market soup. Main courses are simple and hearty, often relying on dairy produce, and include such humble yet delicious national dishes as *rösti* (crispy, fried

grated potato) and *Alpler Magrone* (macaroni cheese with bacon, onions, puréed apples and cinnamon).

Meat-heavy dishes are especially popular in German-speaking areas – often ancient recipes originating in poor, remote regions where the emphasis was on economy and preservation. Look out for tasty cured meats and salamis; sausage and offal dishes such as *Weißwurst* (white veal sausages) and *Leberknodli* (liver dumplings); Zurich's signature dish, *Züri Gschnetzlets* (veal in a cream and mushroom sauce); and game (including chamois, venison and wild boar) in season. Fish is popular throughout the country, with top catches including perch fillets, char, trout, pike, perch, dace and salmon. In Ticino, the cuisine is inspired by neighbouring Italy with an emphasis on pizza, pasta, polenta and risottos.

The culinary capital of Switzerland is Geneva, with its glut of haute cuisine restaurants and some of the finest wines in the land. It is closely followed by Zurich with its trendsetting bistros serving modern interpretations of classic Swiss fare. Recently, other world cuisines have gained a foothold, with fusion cuisine all the rage in the cities' more fashionable restaurants. Vegetarian restaurants are also on the increase, and most menus these days include a handful of suitable options, from simple *rösti* and pasta dishes to more unusual *cardons* (a thistle-like vegetable that tastes like an artichoke, eaten au gratin), wild mushrooms (morel, chanterelle and boletus) and *papet vaudois* (leek casserole).

Those with a sweet tooth will enjoy the many regional treats on dessert menus and the fantastic breads and pastries available in local bakeries.

Taste meringues in Gruyères, smothered with extra-thick double cream, cherry cake in Basel and *kirsch gâteau* in Zug. Look out also for countless chocolate-based puddings, as well as *Apfelküchli* (fried apple slices), *Birchermüsli* (a delicious muesli, fruit and yoghurt mixture, generally eaten as a daytime snack or a light supper) and the ubiquitous *Apfelstrudel* (apple strudel). Try the Vaud speciality, *tarte au vin cuit* (made not with wine but rather a syrupy reduction of pear juice) and the delicious *panettone*, *amaretti*, *torta di pane* (bread cake) and *zabaione* (a kind of custard with sweet wine served with figs) in Ticino.

Etiquette

There is a huge assortment of eating establishments in Switzerland, from

Alpine food offers simple but hearty meals

Tasting wines in Thal, St Gallen

sausage stands and beer cellars to trendy designer bistros and gourmet temples. Eating out is popular, so it is advisable to make a reservation, especially at weekends. In cafés and less expensive restaurants, table sharing is common. Menus already include a service charge of 15 per cent and, although tipping is not necessary, locals usually round up the bill. Food is generally served between noon and 2pm and between 6pm and 9pm (later at weekends).

Swiss wine

Swiss wine is a well-kept secret, surprising in its quality, originality and diversity. The best wines are so sought-after in Switzerland that, beyond the border, they are scarce and expensive. The Romans first brought vines to the country over 2,000 years ago, and some Valaisan red wines are still called *Römerblud* (Romans' blood). The principal vine-growing areas are located in French-speaking Switzerland (Vaud and Valais), although production extends over 15,000ha (37,065 acres) nationwide. Around 50 grape varieties are cultivated, including some found nowhere else such as Petite Arvine, Completer and Amigne whites, and Humagne Rouge and Cornalin reds. The main varieties are the white Chasselas grape (known as 'Fendant' in the Valais), and red Pinot Noir, Gamay and Merlot.

Valaisan wines comprise nearly half of Swiss wines, with specialities including Fendant (a dry white) and Dôle (a smooth red). Principal vineyards of Vaud include La Côte and Le Lavaux on the slopes of Lake Geneva, with well-known light Pinot Noir reds and subtle Chasselas whites produced by Féchy, Epesses, Dézaley and St-Saphorin. Most wine villages have their own *caveau* (cellar) to showcase the local produce, usually open from Easter until October. A list of Lavaux cellars offering tastings is available at *www.lavaux.ch* and of Valaisan cellars at *www.vinsduvalais.ch* (*Open: Easter–Oct*).

Other lesser regions include the slopes of the Neuchâtel, Morat and Bienne lakes, and Satigny near Geneva. In German-speaking Switzerland, Lake Constance produces slightly sparkling whites and Schaffhausen is known for its Blauburgunder reds, while the Rhine Valley (between Chur and Fläsch in Graubünden), warmed by the southern *föhn* wind, produces Pinots Noirs, Rieslings and Chardonnays. With its mild Mediterranean climate, Ticino also produces some outstanding wines, almost exclusively reds, including the heady Merlot del Ticino.

Other beverages

Beer drinking is popular in the German-speaking part of Switzerland, where a Germanic beer-hall culture is strong in the cities. Feldschlösschen is a well-known local producer of Pils and dark beers, while Schützengarten beers are made by the nation's oldest brewery in St Gallen. For spirits, try Schnapps, Appenzeller Alpenbitter (produced from the essence of 67 different flowers) or Xellent (made with Swiss rye and Alpine glacier water). Fruit brandies are a popular *digestif*, often served with or in coffee, and include kirsch (made from cherry pits), Williamine (pears), Damassine (prunes) and Pflümli (plums).

Harvesting grapes can be a tricky business in the Alps!

Entertainment

There's more to Swiss entertainment than yodelling and alphorns. In fact, such traditional forms of entertainment are hard to find these days, except perhaps in the Engadine and Appenzell. Switzerland is less conservative than it was a decade ago, and the major cities each have countless stylish clubs, discos and bars to choose from, ranging from cosy Alpine cabins to sophisticated chill-out bars, and from raucous beer cellars (often with live oompah bands) to mellow jazz joints.

Zurich is the nation's top nightspot – famed for its flamboyant, avant-garde club scene (especially in the Züri-West district) – followed by Lausanne (especially the Flon district) and then Geneva. However, few people party until dawn and nightclubs tend to close at around 1am or 2am. Head to the ski resorts of Villars, Verbier and Zermatt for the liveliest après-ski scene, or rub shoulders with the rich and the wannabes at St Moritz and Gstaad. The main arenas for blockbuster pop concerts, drawing top international superstars, are the indoor Hallenstadion in Zurich, Bern's outdoor Stade de Suisse, Geneva's Arena and St-Jakobs Arena in Lausanne. There are also several summer rock festivals including the massive Paleo in Nyon (*www.paleo.ch*).

Cinema

Cinema is extremely popular in Switzerland, with most city-centre cinemas showing the latest releases in the original version with subtitles. During summer months, open-air cinemas are set up in Bern, Basel, Zurich, Lausanne, Geneva, Lugano and Locarno (Europe's largest open-air cinema, *see p173*). The Geneva Film Festival each October screens the work of up-and-coming European talent (*www.genevafilmfestival.org*).

Fireworks at the Fêtes de Genève

Classical music and dance

Every main city has at least one symphony orchestra and classical music festival, as well as chamber concerts and recitals, staged in various indoor and outdoor venues. Top concert halls include Zurich's Tonhalle (*see p157*), the KKL in Luzern (*see p169*) and Victoria Hall in Geneva (*see p162*), home of the prestigious Orchestre de la Suisse Romande, which performs in Geneva and Lausanne. The most famous musical festivals are the International Luzern Festival (*see p19*) and the Montreux International Jazz Festival (*see p19*). For modern dance, it's hard to beat the highly acclaimed Béjart Ballet in Lausanne.

Theatre

Switzerland boasts an impressive programme of performing arts, festivals and cultural events throughout the year, especially in Zurich with its world-renowned Opernhaus (Opera House) (*see p156*) and Schauspielhaus (the nation's largest theatre and one of the most influential in the German-speaking world) (*see p156*). Lausanne's Théâtre de Vidy is another major venue, famed throughout Europe for its innovative productions (in French) (*see p163*). Puppet theatre is especially popular with younger visitors (*see p143*).

Listings and tickets

To find out what's on when, ask at the local tourist office, look out for free

Chill out at the Montreux Jazz Festival

listings newspapers and magazines in bars, hotel lobbies and railway stations, or check in the culture section of the local newspapers (*see p149*).

Tickets are best purchased from the relevant box office at each venue, or by phone or internet from agencies including *www.ticketcorner.com*, *www.starticket.ch* and *www.tictec.ch*. Some tourist offices and department stores offer advance bookings, and there are special ticketing centres in most towns and cities, including BiZZ in Zurich (*Tel: (044) 221 22 83*) and FNAC in Basel, Fribourg, Geneva and Lausanne (*www.fnac.ch*).

Shopping

From the ultimate Swiss army knife and quality Swiss handicrafts through to classical watches, extravagant jewellery and international haute couture, or even just a bar of chocolate or some cheese, whatever you are looking for, you will find it in Switzerland – a veritable shoppers' paradise that never fails to delight.

Swiss made

Shopaholics will simply adore Switzerland, with its huge variety of shopping experiences – from chic city department stores and deluxe designer boutiques to lively flea markets, village stores and farmers' markets. The big cities thrive on the world's well-known brands, but keep a lookout for Swiss design and fun Swiss-made

Swiss army knives are popular gifts

souvenirs too. Switzerland is world renowned for its well-crafted, well-designed merchandise, and the very best can be found in branches of Heimatwerk throughout the country. Other popular Swiss brands to look out for include Caran d'Ache – the world's first water-soluble brand of colouring pencil, Victorinox Swiss army knives (*see p101*), affordable Swatch® watches and current trend-setting labels – Freitag (hip, courier-style satchels made from recycled truck tarpaulins) and Alprausch, with its fashionable urban-, beach- and snow-wear.

Where to shop

Zurich is Switzerland's undisputed shopping capital. Its celebrated Bahnhofstrasse is one of the world's top shopping miles – where all the Zürchers come to promenade and shop. It contains Switzerland's most sophisticated department stores, top designer boutiques (including the world's largest outlet of Bally), the favourite chocolate shop of the Swiss (Sprüngli), and some of the most exclusive jewellers and watchmakers in the world. By contrast, in the Altstadt and Niederdorf districts, there is an abundance of interior design stores, artisans' galleries and antique shops, as well as quirky trendsetting boutiques selling everything imaginable from cheese to children's books.

Shopping in Geneva is also a joy, with its trendy boutiques in the Old Town, and more sophisticated label shopping in and around chic rue du Rhône. Shopping in Lugano has a distinctly Italianate flair, strongly influenced by fashions from nearby Milan. Tradition and modernity go hand in hand in Luzern, from the traditional Conditorei Heini cake shop with its celebrated 'Luzern Raindrops' (cherry-liqueur filled chocolate drops) to the flagship store of the leading Swiss watch and jewellery retailer, Bucherer.

Bern's historic centre also offers a wonderful shopping experience. Its tiny, one-off boutiques, designer fashions and exclusive gift shops are housed in grand arcaded town houses, making shopping here a pleasure come rain or shine. Some shops are veritable treasure troves, located in beautiful, vaulted cellars beneath the cobbled streets. And there are plenty of ubiquitous souvenir shops with an amusing selection of beer steins, nostalgic music boxes, kitsch fondue pots, Swiss army knives and cowbells.

Swiss precision engineering

Alpine shopping

Shopping has become a popular après-ski pastime at many of the larger resorts, with Swiss-made skis, snowboards, gadgets and gizmos, and the very latest sporting fashions. The ultimate shopping resort is Gstaad – where retail therapy is taken as seriously as the skiing. Here, alongside designer stores and jewellers, are some unusual boutiques that give the village its appeal.

Tax-free shopping

For purchases over CHF300 (in one shop) by non-residents, Swiss Value Added Tax (VAT) is reimbursable by using the Global Refund system. Contact *www.globalrefund.com* for further details.

Sport and leisure

The Swiss love the great outdoors. They are more environmentally conscious than many of their neighbouring European countries, and they devote much of their recreation time to sports and an outdoor lifestyle. With such beautiful countryside, walking, hiking and cycling rank among the most popular outdoor pursuits. Horse riding is popular in rural regions, and the nation has some of the most scenic golf courses in Europe.

Adventure sports

The Swiss are keen on high-adrenalin sports, including rock climbing, high-altitude trekking (with a guide), canyoning, white-water rafting, hang-gliding, paragliding, microlighting, downhill mountain biking and bungee jumping. The Verzasca dam in Ticino is the site of the world's biggest bungee jump, made famous in the James Bond adventure movie *Goldeneye*.

Water sports

There has been a revival in water sports ever since 2003, when Swiss-financed Alinghi became the first European team to win sailing's oldest trophy, the 150-year-old America's Cup. Swimming is popular in lakeside towns and cities with their lovely lakeside beaches and lidos. The larger lakes offer boat hire, from pedalos to motorboats and sailing craft, and Silvaplana is a top windsurfing and kiteboarding centre (*www.surfclub-silvaplana.ch*).

Winter sports

Skiing reigns supreme in winter months, with 207 downhill resorts (mainly in Valais, the Bernese Oberland and Graubünden) and over 5,000km (3,100 miles) of marked cross-country pistes. Snowboarding is a huge craze. Other snow pursuits include tobogganing, curling and ice-skating; novelty activities such as snow-biking, dog sledding (*see pp106–7*) and ski-jöring; and extreme sports – ice-wall climbing, ski touring, glacier hiking and heli-skiing.

Passes and equipment

Passes for cable cars and ski lifts vary in price from resort to resort, and most offer a variety of half-day and multi-day discounts. There are ski and snowboarding schools (*www.snowsports.ch*) attached to most resorts, and equipment, from skis to mountain bikes, can be rented in most resorts. InterSport (*www.intersport.ch*) and SwissRent (*www.swissrent.com*) are reliable nationwide rental outlets.

Spas and thermal springs

Spas, health clinics and wellness centres are extremely popular in Switzerland, with pampering ranging from high-tech 'scientific rejuvenation' at Switzerland's most celebrated spa, Clinique La Prairie, to an Appenzeller mud bath at Natur-Moorbad Gonten (*www. naturmoorbad.ch, see p36*) or a decadent 'hot chocolate wrap' in Wienacht (*www.hotel-seeblick.ch*).

Public 'wellness baths' offer a combination of indoor and outdoor natural spring pools for swimming and relaxation. Leukerbad, in Valais, has Europe's largest (and highest) thermal baths (*www.leukerbad.com*).

Sport and leisure

Adrenaline junkies are well catered for, with sports such as paragliding on offer

Other centres can be found at Lavey-les-Bains (*www.lavey-les-bains.ch*), Saillon (*www.bainsdesaillon.ch*) and Bad Ragaz (*www.resortragaz.ch*).

The state-of-the-art granite and quartzite complex of Therme Vals (*www.therme-vals.ch*) is arguably the best thermal spa in Switzerland, closely followed by Spa Bogn Engadina (Engadine Spa Baths, *www.scuol.ch*) at Scuol, which also provides the full indoor–outdoor bathing experience, and a Roman Spa.

Hotel spas are currently all the rage in Switzerland. Among the top ones are the spa at La Réserve Genève Hotel (*www.lareserve.ch*), the spa at Victoria-Jungfrau Grand Hotel, Interlaken (*www.victoria-jungfrau.ch*, *see p160*), the St Moritz SPA (*www.kempinski-stmoritz.com*), Zurich's new Dolder Grand Spa (*www.the doldergrand.com*) and the Bergoase Spa at the Tschuggen Grand Hotel (*www.tschuggen.ch*) in Arosa, if only for its extraordinary Alpine architecture by Mario Botta (*see p56*).

Spectator sports

Switzerland hosts a number of world-class sporting events throughout the year that draw spectators from around the world. Ice hockey and football attract the largest crowds. Football (*www.football.ch*) has grown in popularity since the nation won a surprising play-off against Turkey to qualify for the 2006 World Cup. Top local clubs include FC Basel and the Zurich Grasshoppers. Zurich is the headquarters of FIFA, the world football governing body, and the nation jointly hosted Euro 2008 with Austria. It was the largest sporting event ever staged in Switzerland.

Ice hockey is fast and furious, and always a thrill to watch. The top teams include Davos, the Kloten Flyers, Bern and Lugano. The Spengler Cup international ice hockey tournament (*www.spenglercup.ch*) in Davos in late December is a highlight of the season. The Château-d'Oex Hot Air Ballooning Week attracts 80 balloons from 15 countries and is one of the most magnificent spectacles in the Alps. The Velogemel (snowbike) World Championships are staged in Grindelwald each February.

St Moritz holds a variety of unusual sporting events each January: horse racing on snow (*www.whiteturf.ch*), show jumping on snow (*www.stmoritz-concours.ch*), snow polo (*www.polostmoritz.com*), snow golf (*www.silvaplana.ch*) and even cricket on ice (*www.cricket-on-ice.com*). Yet the real crowd-pullers are the Bobsleigh (*www.olympia-bobrun.ch*) and Cresta Run (*www.cresta-run.com*) events, staged between mid-December and February, when even the race training draws enthusiastic spectators.

The most prestigious winter sports event is the Lauberhorn World Cup ski race (*www.lauberhorn.ch*) – the longest and fastest downhill run in the world at 4.5km (2³/₄ miles) with skiers reaching speeds close to 160kph (100mph). The race has taken place in Wengen every January since 1930 and attracts around 30,000 spectators each year.

Swiss tennis has undergone a renaissance ever since Basel-born tennis ace Roger Federer became the world's number one player in 2004. Top annual tennis events include the Swiss Open, held in Gstaad in July (*www.allianzsuisseopengstaad.com*), the Swiss Indoors (*www.swissindoors.ch*) at Basel, and the Zurich Open (*www.zurichopen.net*) in October.

Other major sporting events include the CSI international indoor showjumping tournament in Zurich in January–February; the Tour de Suisse (*www.tds.ch*) and the Swiss Inline Cup (*www.swiss-inline-cup.ch*), the world's largest inline marathon, in Zurich in June; the European Masters golf tournament in Crans-Montana (*www.omegaeuropeanmasters.com*), and World Class Zurich (*www.weltklasse.ch*), the highlight of the international athletics calendar (late Aug–Sept).

Tickets

Tickets for most sporting events can be obtained directly from the relevant box office at each venue. Alternatively, you can book by phone or via the internet at various agencies, including *www.ticketcorner.com*, *www.starticket.ch* and *www.tictec.ch*. Most cities have ticket-purchasing centres, including FNAC Rive in Geneva (Rive 16. *Tel: (022) 816 12 12. www.fnac.ch*); the Service Culturel Migros-Vaud in Lausanne (*rue de Genève 35. Tel: (021) 318 71 71*) and BiZZ Central Ticket Office in Zurich (*Stadthausquai 17. Tel: (044) 221 22 83*). Contact the local tourist office for further information.

Tennis is ever popular, thanks to local hero Roger Federer

Children

Switzerland is a paradise for children, with plenty of outdoor activities, fun museums and other appealing attractions, not to mention fabulous toy shops and chocolate shops, which are always good for a treat. Most restaurants and cafés welcome children, and many offer special menus, portions and high chairs; Swiss Railways offers a special discounted Family Card (see p126) and family carriages on many of its intercity trains; playgrounds abound and everywhere is spotlessly clean!

Accommodation

Children are spoiled for choice, from campsites to igloos, alpine huts or even 'sleeping on straw' (*see pp128–9*). Contact Switzerland Tourism for details of 39 special Kids' Hotels, with play areas, tasty menus and fun accommodation, enabling parents to relax (*www.myswitzerland.com*).

Circuses and zoos

The Swiss National Circus Knie (*www.knie.ch*) regularly tours the country. Its Circus Museum, at Rapperswil near Zurich, provides a fascinating insight into its animal training, while the nearby Knies Children's Zoo (*www.knieskinderzoo.ch*) is popular with younger children. Zurich's Zoo (*www.zoo.ch*) contains a vast re-creation of a Masoala rainforest. The zoo at Servion (*www.zoo-servion.ch*), near Lausanne, and Basel Zoo (*www.zoobasel.ch*) are also worth a visit, and all children adore Bern's resident bears in the city's celebrated Bärengraben (*see p55*).

Excursions, sports and outdoor activities

Walks for the young include the Marmot Trail at Saas Fee (*see p120*), the Heidi Path near Maienfeld, the Heidi Flower Trail and the Schellen Ursli Path near St Moritz, recounting the celebrated Engadine story of *Ursli's Bell*. The open-air museum at Ballenberg is also a fun day out (*see p62*), combined with the Gnome Path at nearby Meiringen (*www.muggestutz.ch*).

Little ones adore the different types of transport, especially up the mountain tops, to the ice palace at the top of the Jungfrau (*see p61*), or to the Swiss Vapeur Park at Le Bouveret (near Montreux) – one of Europe's finest miniature steam rail parks (*www.swissvapeur.ch*). Older children may prefer hiring in-line skates or bikes to explore the countryside. Football fans will enjoy touring Bern's Stade de Suisse, and Parc Aventure's woodland assault courses at Aigle in Valais, and at Signal de Bougy near Geneva, challenge even the most adventurous teenagers (*www.parc-aventure.ch*).

Winter is a time for snowmen and snowball fights, ice-skating, tobogganing and even skiing lessons (from age three in most resorts). Some of the best toboggan runs are at Leysin (*see p163*), Meiringen, Andermatt, Klosters and Grindelwald – the longest toboggan run in Europe.

The best water parks are Aquaparc at Le Bouveret (*www.aquaparc.ch*) and Alpamare (*www.alpamare.ch*) at Pfäffikon – Europe's largest indoor water park. Further fun excursions are to the underground Trümmelbach waterfalls near Mürren (*www.truemmelbachfaelle.ch*), or to Europe's largest underground lake (*www.lac-souterrain.com*) near Sion.

Museums and theatres

Older children enjoy Luzern's Swiss Transport Museum (*see p93*), the International Red Cross Museum in Geneva (*see p68*), the Swiss Games Museum near Vevey (*see p74*), and the amazing hands-on Technorama science centre at Winterthur (*www.technorama.ch*). Younger children especially like Zurich's Toy Museum (*www.zuercher-spielzeugmusuem.ch*), the children's art centre at Bern's Zentrum Paul Klee (*see p53*) and the mirror maze at Luzern's Glacier Garden (*www.gletschergarten.ch*).

Children's theatre and puppet shows are also popular, especially at the Children's Theatre Lausanne (*www.regart.ch/tpel*), Zurich's Theater Stadelhofen (*www.theater-stadelhofen ch*) and the Berner Puppentheater (*www.berner-puppentheater.ch*, *see p159*).

Some trails, like this one near the Aletsch Glacier, are suitable for all ages

Children

Essentials

Arriving & departing
By air
Switzerland has two major international airports – Zurich's Kloten Airport (*www.zurich-airport.com*) and Geneva International Airport (*www.gva.ch*). There are also three secondary airports – EuroAirport Basel (*www.euroairport. com*), Bern-Belp (*www.flughafenbern.ch*) and Lugano Airport (*www.lugano-airport.ch*), which are growing in popularity, especially with low-cost carriers. There is also a host of airstrips around the country, including the Aeroport de Sion (a popular departure point for mountain tours; *www. sionairport.ch*) and Engadin Airport (*www.engadin-airport.ch*) at Samedan, the highest airport in Europe (1,707m/ 5,600ft), where royals, aristocrats and hedonists fly into St Moritz.

Zurich's Kloten Airport, located 11km (7 miles) north of the city, is among the busiest airports in Europe, and is Switzerland's largest, with one terminal serviced by over 100 different airlines, mostly offering scheduled services. Swiss International Air Lines (*www.swiss.com*), the national carrier, is the main operator, followed by British Airways (*www.britishairways.com*), Lufthansa (*www.lufthansa.ch*) and Air France (*www.airfrance.ch*). Transatlantic airlines include American Airlines (*www.aa.com*) and Delta (*www.delta.com*). Geneva International Airport has one terminal and is located 5km (3 miles) north of Geneva. The main carrier here is Swiss International Air Lines (*www.swiss.com*).

Both Zurich and Geneva airports have excellent facilities, including banks and cash dispensers, pharmacies, post offices, business centres, children's play zones, car rental (including Hertz, Avis, Europcar, Budget and Sixt) and a host of bars, cafés and shops full of last-minute gift ideas.

By road
If you do not wish to fly or drive, coach travel is a good alternative, with reasonably priced fares and discounts for travellers under 25, over 60 and those with disabilities. Contact Eurolines (*www.eurolines.com*) for further information.

Driving in Switzerland is relatively straightforward, with a comprehensive network of motorways (labelled 'A' roads for *Autobahn/Autoroute/ Autostrada*) and main roads (labelled 'N' for *Nationalstrasse* or 'E' for European roads). As a general rule, names of towns are used for navigation on the roads, rather than the highway numbers, which are rarely seen. Before arriving in Switzerland, you need to purchase a *vignette* (annual motorway tax, *see p127*). Seatbelts are compulsory in the front and the back, as are car seats for children under the age of seven. Keep to the speed limits – 120kph (74mph) on motorways, 80kph (50mph) on main roads and 50kph (31mph) around town – radar traps are frequent, and speeding and other traffic offences are subject to on-the-spot fines. There are extremely severe penalties for drink-driving. Try to avoid driving at rush hour (*Mon–Fri 7–8.30am & 4.30–6.30pm; Fri evenings & Sun evenings, especially during winter*). It is always advisable to check the road conditions before setting out on any long journey (*www.strasseninfo.ch*).

By rail

It is easy to travel to Switzerland from mainland Europe by train. Contact Rail Europe (*www.raileurope.com*) and the SBB in Switzerland (*www.sbb.ch*) for further information.

Customs

Visitors from Europe may import 200 cigarettes, 50 cigars or 250g of tobacco. Visitors from non-European countries may import twice as much. For alcohol, the limits are the same for everyone: 1 litre of spirits (over 15 per cent alcohol content), 2 litres of wine (less than 15 per cent alcohol). Gifts up to the value of CHF100 may also be imported.

Switzerland is one of Europe's last countries offering duty-free shopping, with savings of up to 20 per cent on perfumes and cosmetics, up to 30 per cent on wines and spirits, and up to 50 per cent on tobacco products.

Electricity

Switzerland's electricity supply is at 220V, 50Hz. Swiss sockets are generally recessed, and plugs are round, flat or hexagonally shaped with two pins. British appliances need a plug adaptor, and North American appliances also need a 220–110V transformer.

Internet

If you prefer to email, many hotels now offer internet and wireless access, and there are internet cafés around the towns, cities and larger resorts, although these can be quite expensive. Most public phone boxes have an electronic phonebook, from which you can send short emails worldwide for as little as CHF1.50.

Money

Switzerland's currency is the Swiss franc (CHF), which is made up of 100 centimes (also called *Rappen* in German and *centesimi* in Italian). Banknotes are available in denominations of 10, 20, 50, 100, 500 and 1,000 francs, and coins are minted as 5, 10, 20 and 50 centimes, and also 1, 2 and 5 francs.

Given Switzerland's central location in Europe, prices are often also marked in euros and many of the larger shops will accept euro notes, although you should expect your change to be in Swiss francs. Credit cards are widely accepted. Traveller's cheques are rarely used and are not usually accepted in shops. As one of the world's main banking centres, there are plenty of banks to choose from for currency exchange, as well as bureaux de change booths at the main airports and major train stations. ATMs (cash machines) are common – usually accessible 24 hours a day and with multilingual instructions for use. Most bank cards are accepted for withdrawing Swiss francs, provided you know your PIN (personal identification number) and some will also dispense euros.

Opening hours

Most shops (including pharmacies) are open Monday to Friday from 9.30am to noon and from 2pm to 6.30pm, and on Saturday from 8.30am to noon. However, in the cities most shops stay open during the lunch hour, and until 4pm or 5pm on Saturdays. Some shops close on Monday mornings, and some cities have late-night shopping on Thursdays until 8pm, including Bern, Geneva and Zurich. At large train stations with adjoining shopping malls, the opening hours are usually longer, including on Sundays.

Banks are generally open Monday to Friday from 8.30am to 4.30pm (until 6pm on Thursdays in some cities). Post office opening times are customarily Monday to Friday from 7.30am to 6pm and on Saturdays from 8am to 11am, although main city post offices may open longer. Museum and gallery opening times vary across the country. Many open on Sundays and close for at least one other day a week, often on a Monday.

Passports and visas

Citizens of Australia, Canada, New Zealand, South Africa, the UK and the USA need a valid passport to enter Switzerland. You are expected to carry your passport at all times during your visit by law. A visa is required if the duration of the stay exceeds 90 days.

Pharmacies

Medicines can be obtained by your local pharmacy, which are easily identifiable by the sign of a green cross on a white background. They dispense over-the-counter and prescription-only medicines. Medicines in Switzerland are generally very expensive, so it is wise to pack a small supply of painkillers, cold remedies and any other small items you may need.

Post

Switzerland's postal service (*Swiss Post. www.swisspost.ch*) is fast and reliable. There are three methods to send international mail: Urgent (for same-day or next-day international deliveries), Priority or A-Post (which takes between two and four working days to Europe and around seven days elsewhere), and Economy or B-Post (four to eight days to Europe and seven to twelve days for other destinations).

Within Switzerland, deliveries are either A-Post (delivered the next working day) or B-Post (taking three working days). Stamps can be purchased at post offices and sometimes at newspaper kiosks. It costs CHF1.30 to send an airmail letter (up to 20g) within Europe or CHF1.80 to the rest of the world.

Public holidays

The following days are national holidays in Switzerland:

1 Jan – New Year's Day
Mar/Apr – Good Friday, Easter Sunday and Monday
40th day after Easter – Ascension day
7th week after Easter – Whit Sunday and Monday
1 Aug – National Day
25 Dec – Christmas Day
26 Dec – St Stephen's Day

Some cantons also have their own special holidays and religious observances, including Labour Day (1 May), Assumption (15 Aug) and All Saints' Day (1 Nov).

Smoking

There is no national smoking policy. However, each canton has its own smoking regulations. In Geneva, for instance, or in the canton of Graubünden, smoking is banned in all public areas (restaurants, bars, etc) while in the canton of Zurich, smoking has been outlawed only in public buildings.

Suggested reading and media
Fiction

Daisy Miller by Henry James, set at Lake Geneva and Château de Chillon.

Dr Fischer of Geneva by Graham Greene is a short but revelatory love story with a few surprising twists.

History and travelogues

Switzerland Unwrapped by Mitya New takes a look at Swiss culture.
Ticking Along with the Swiss by Diana Dicks is an amusing anthology of tales from travellers and expats.
When the Alps Cast Their Spell; Mountaineers of the Golden Age of Alpinism by Trevor Braham documents Alpine exploration in the 19th century.
William Tell: Portrait of a Legend by Walter Dettwiler.

Humour

Laughing Along with the Swiss by Paul Bilton contains witty narratives on various aspects of Swiss life.
Once Upon an Alp, Lend Me Your Alphorn and *Take Me to Your Chalet* by Eugene Epstein analyse the oddities of Swiss life and its many clichés.

Newspapers

Somewhat surprisingly for such a small country, Switzerland has over 200 different newspapers. The majority, however, are simple, provincial news-sheets. The main papers are the *Neue Zürcher Zeitung* (NZZ) and the *Tages Anzeiger* (in German), *Le Temps* and *La Tribune de Genève* (in French) and the *Corriere del Ticino* (in Italian). Of the various tabloids, *Blick* (in German) is the nation's best-seller.

Foreign newspapers are pricey and are usually on sale the same day in main train stations and in some city kiosks.

Reference

Living and Working in Switzerland by David Hampshire.
Walking Switzerland the Swiss Way by Marcia and Philip Lieberman.

Television and radio

Switzerland has seven main terrestrial television stations available nationwide, plus a variety of local stations for each area. Most hotels now offer satellite television, providing channels in various languages, including CNN and BBC Prime.

The BBC World Service in English is available on 648MW, and BBC world news is broadcast on World Radio Geneva (88.4FM). Full details of all TV and radio stations are available at *www.srg.ch*

Useful websites

www.myswitzerland.com Switzerland Tourism's official website.
www.swissinfo.ch National news.
www.myswissalps.com Useful information on sports activities and alpine areas.
www.sbb.ch The Swiss Railway website.
www.swissmade.com Shopping website.

Tax

VAT (value added tax) (MwSt in German, TVA in French and IVA in Italian) is added to goods and services at a rate of 7.6 per cent, except in hotels where it is only 3.6 per cent. Non-residents can claim tax back on purchases over CHF300. Refunds can be claimed by post, from major border crossings and at Geneva and Zurich airports, as long as you have all the paperwork from the shop (*see p137*).

Airport arrival and departure tax is included in the price of the airline ticket.

Telephones

The country code for phoning Switzerland is *41*. To phone from abroad, first dial your international access code (usually *00*), then the national code (*41*) followed by the regional code and then the individual number (usually 7 digits).

To phone home from Switzerland, dial the outgoing code *00*, followed by the country code:
Australia + *61*
New Zealand + *64*
UK + *44*
USA and Canada + *1*
South Africa + *27*

Dial *1141* for the international operator, and *1811* for national directory enquiries.

Switzerland's main telephone provider is Swisscom (*www. swisscom.com*). Public phone boxes can be found in all towns and cities, and are straightforward to use, with polyglot instructions. All boxes take major credit cards and coins. For collect calls to

Australia, Canada, Japan, the UK and the USA, and worldwide calls with a credit card, dial 0800 265 532, wait for the prompt then dial 1 for English or 0 for the operator.

Mobile phones

Most mobile phones on European networks will work in Switzerland. Alternatively, you can buy prepaid local SIM cards from Orange (*www.orange.ch*), Sunrise (*www.sunrise.ch*) and Swisscom Mobile (*www.swisscom-mobile.ch*). These can be bought from a nationwide chain of shops called Mobile Zone (*www.mobilezone.ch*). You will need your passport when you buy one.

Time

Zurich follows Central European Time (CET), which is 1 hour ahead of Greenwich Mean Time (GMT + 1). When it's noon in Zurich, this is the time back home:
Australia: Eastern Standard 8pm, Central Standard 7.30pm, Western Standard 6pm
South Africa: noon
New Zealand: 10pm
UK: 11am
USA: Eastern 6am, Central 5am, Mountain 4am, Pacific 3am, Alaska 2am.

Toilets

Public toilets are generally clean and free, although some do have a small charge (ranging from CHF0.20 to CHF2 in the smart MrClean toilet and shower facilities in main train stations).

Travellers with disabilities

The standard of facilities for travellers with disabilities is high in Switzerland, especially on public transport. Special taxi services are available and specially adapted vehicles can be hired from various car rental companies (*www.mietauto.ch*) throughout Switzerland. Foreign visitors clearly displaying a disability ID issued in their country can park on designated disabled parking spaces. To receive help getting on or off a train at one of the 160 stations nationwide with special facilities, phone the SBB Call Center Handicap (*Tel: 0800 007 102 toll-free. Open: 6am–10pm*) one hour before the train is due to leave. Further information is available online (*www.sbb.ch*) or in the brochure *Travellers with a Handicap*, available from any train station. There is also a volunteer service at all major train stations, called Compagna (*Eschenstrasse 1, St Gallen. Tel: (071) 220 16 07. www.compagna.ch*), which will transfer people from trains to taxis and even accompany them further if necessary.

Many Swiss hotels have specific facilities for guests with special needs, including wheelchair-friendly rooms. Switzerland Tourism (*www.myswitzerland.com*) can provide full details of suitable hotels. Many excursions are suited to wheelchair users. Contact Mobility International Switzerland for further information (*Froburgstrasse 4, Olten. Tel: (062) 206 88 35. www.mis-ch.ch*).

Language

Switzerland has three official languages. German is spoken by around 64 per cent of the population, French by 19 per cent and Italian by 8 per cent. It also has one 'semi-official' language, Rhaeto-Romansh (see p108), spoken by less than 1 per cent of the country in the Engadine region. English is widely spoken – it is taught in most schools (before French in some parts of German-speaking Switzerland) and especially in businesses spanning the different language regions.

Swiss German or Schweizer Deutsch (Schwizerdütsch in local dialect) is spoken in 17 cantons, in central and eastern Switzerland. It differs from standard High German or Hochdeutsch (Hochdütsch) in phonology, vocabulary and grammar (especially verb forms). High German is widely used for writing, but Swiss German dialects are used from day to day and can be extremely difficult to understand, even for native German-speakers.

French is spoken in the Suisse Romande, the western part of the country, in Geneva, Jura, Neuchâtel and Vaud cantons. Swiss French is essentially the same as standard French, although there are a few differences in vocabulary and pronunciation. Three cantons – Bern, Fribourg and Valais – are bilingual, speaking both French and German. They are split by the Röstigraben, an invisible internal border between the country's two main language regions.

Italian is spoken in Ticino and southern parts of Graubünden. There are few differences between the Ticines dialect and standard Italian. Three languages are spoken in Graubünden – German, Italian and, in some remote mountain valleys, Romansh. This Latin-based language is over 2,000 years old and, although so few people speak it, those that do are proud of their culture and are striving to preserve it.

NUMBERS

English	German	French	Italian
1	eins	un	uno
2	zwei	deux	due
3	drei	trois	tre
4	vier	quatre	quattro
5	fünf	cinq	cinque
6	sechs	six	sei
7	sieben	sept	sette
8	acht	huit	otto
9	neun	neuf	nove
10	zehn	dix	dieci

English	German	French	Italian
Yes	Ja	Oui	Sì
No	Nein	Non	No
Hello	Guten Tag	Bonjour	Buongiorno
Goodbye	Auf Wiedersehen	Au revoir	Arrivederci
Good morning/ afternoon/evening	Guten Morgen/ Tag/Abend	Bonjour/bon après- midi/bonsoir	Buongiorno/buon pomeriggio/ buona sera
Excuse me	Entschuldigung	Excusez-moi	Mi scusi
I (don't) understand	Ich verstehe (nicht)	Je (ne) comprends (pas)	(non) capisco
Do you speak English?	Sprechen Sie Englisch?	Parlez-vous anglais?	Parla inglese?
I come from Britain/America	Ich komme aus Großbritannien/ Amerika	Je viens de Grande- Bretagne/ des États-Unis	Vengo dal Gran Bretagna/Stati Uniti
opening hours	Öffnungseiten	heures d'ouverture	orari d'apertura
open/closed	offen/geschlossen	ouvert/fermé	aperto/chiuso
Call a doctor/ the police	Rufen Sie einen Arzt/ Rufen Sie die Polizei!	Appelez un médecin/ la police!	Chiami un medico/la polizia!
I'd like to buy...	Ich möchte … kaufen	Je voudrais acheter…	Vorrei comprare…
How much is it?	Wie viel kostet das?	Ça coûte combien?	Quanto costa?
Where is a hotel/ a bank/a pharmacy/ the post office/ the train station/ the toilet/ the tourist office?	Wo ist ein Hotel/ eine Bank/eine Apotheke/die Post/ der Bahnhof/ die Toilette/ die Touristauskunft?	Où est un hôtel/ une banque/une pharmacie/la poste/ la gare/ les toilettes/l'office de tourisme?	Dov'è un hotel/ una banca/un apotheke/l'ufficio postale/stazione di treno/la toletta/ l'ufficio di turismo?
Too... big/small	zu... groß/klein	trop … grand/petit	troppo …grande/ piccolo
new/old	neu/alt	nouveau/vieux	nuovo/vecchio
clean/dirty	sauber/schmutzig	propre/sale	pulito/sporco
quiet/noisy	ruhig/laut	calme/bruyant	silenzioso/rumoroso
hot/cold	warm/kalt	chaud/froid	caldo/freddo

DAYS OF THE WEEK

Monday	Montag	lundi	lunedì
Tuesday	Dienstag	mardi	martedì
Wednesday	Mittwoch	mercredi	mercoledì
Thursday	Donnerstag	jeudi	giovedì
Friday	Freitag	vendredi	venerdì
Saturday	Samstag	samedi	sabato
Sunday	Sonntag	dimanche	domenica

Emergencies

Telephone numbers

Police: *117*
Fire: *118*
Ambulance: *144*
Crisis line: *143*
Highway rescue: *140*
Mountain Air Rescue: *1414* or *1415*

Health care

Switzerland has one of the best health care systems in the world, with modern, well-equipped hospitals and superb nursing care. There is no free state health service in Switzerland, so make sure you have adequate health insurance prior to your visit. Citizens of EU countries are entitled to reduced price, sometimes free, medical treatment on presentation of a valid European Health Insurance Card (EHIC). On top of this, private medical insurance is still advised and is essential for all non-EU visitors. Dental care, except emergency accident treatment, is not available free of charge and should be covered by private medical insurance.

If you require a particular prescription medication, take an adequate supply with you, as it may not

Take care when hiking – steep drops and fast-moving water can catch you unawares

be available locally, and a letter of authorisation from your doctor. Should you become seriously ill, lists of local doctors, dentists and hospitals can be found in telephone directories, or ask your hotel reception or your consulate. In a medical emergency, dial 144. Every town has at least one 24-hour pharmacy. Ask the local tourist office or your hotel reception for details.

Swiss food should present no health risk to travellers. Tap and fountain water is safe to drink (unless marked *Kein Trinkwasser* or *eau non potable*, meaning 'not drinking water'), but it is advisable not to drink from Alpine water sources without first purifying it. Nappies, baby food and formula milk can easily be bought in supermarkets. However, if you have a preferred brand, bring a supply with you.

Crime and safety

Switzerland is essentially a safe country, but although crime rates are relatively low, it is advisable to take common-sense precautions against petty crime: don't carry excess cash, use the hotel safe for valuable goods, beware of pickpockets in crowded places and stick to well-lit populated areas by night.

Police (*Polizei* in German, *police* in French, *polizia* in Italian) are grouped into cantonal authorities, although there are federal police and city police too. If you are involved in any crime, go to the nearest police station to file a report (if only for insurance purposes).

Mountain safety and emergencies

When hiking in the mountains, make sure you are well equipped, as weather conditions can change rapidly, even in midsummer. Wear sturdy walking boots, and make sure you pack sufficient food and drink, sunscreen, sunglasses, waterproofs, plenty of warm clothing, a whistle, a torch, a map and binoculars in your backpack. Switzerland experiences about 10,000 avalanches a year, and around 200 people are killed by them annually in the Alps, mostly in avalanches that they themselves have caused. It is therefore imperative that warnings are heeded, and local advice sought before leaving prepared runs.

Embassies and consulates

Australia
Chemin des Fins 2, Grand-Saconnex, Geneva. Tel: (022) 799 91 00. www.australia.ch

Canada
Kirchenfeldstrasse 88, Bern. Tel: (031) 357 32 00. www.canada-ambassade.ch

New Zealand
Chemin des Fins 2, Grand-Saconnex, Geneva. Tel: (022) 929 03 50.

South Africa
Alpenstrasse 29, Bern. Tel: (031) 350 13 13. www.southafrica.ch

UK
Thunstrasse 50, Bern. Tel: (031) 359 77 00. www.britain-in-switzerland.ch

USA
Sulgeneckstrasse 19, Bern. Tel: (031) 357 70 11. http://bern.usembassy.gov

Directory

Accommodation price guide

Prices of accommodation are based on an average double room including breakfast. Please note that prices may vary considerably from season to season.

★	Under CHF150
★★	CHF150–CHF250
★★★	CHF250–CHF400
★★★★	Over CHF400

Eating out price guide

Prices are based on an average meal for one, excluding drinks.

★	Under CHF25
★★	CHF25–CHF50
★★★	CHF50–CHF75
★★★★	Over CHF75

NORTHEAST SWITZERLAND

Appenzell

ACCOMMODATION

Adler ★★

Stay in a traditional 'Appenzeller' bedroom, decorated with beautiful hand-painted rustic furniture.
Adlerplatz 5.
Tel: (071) 787 13 89.
www.adlerhotel.ch

Säntis ★★★

Appenzell's top hotel is at the heart of the action, overlooking the town's main square, and in a traditional building with a beautifully painted exterior. Ask for a room with a four-poster bed.
Landsgemeindeplatz 3.
Tel: (071) 788 11 11.
www.saentis-appenzell.ch

EATING OUT

Hof ★

Delicious cheese dishes, *rösti* and other popular Swiss fare.
Engelgasse 4.
Tel: (071) 787 40 30.
www.gasthaus-hof.ch.
Open: noon–10pm.

Kreuzlingen

EATING OUT

Seegarten ★★★

An upmarket fish restaurant on the shores of Lake Constance.
Promenadenstrasse 40.
Tel: (071) 688 28 77.
www.seegarten.ch. Closed: Mon (and Tue Sept–May).

Schaffhausen

EATING OUT

Fischerzunft ★★★★

One of the country's top restaurants, on the banks of the River Rhine, serving exotic French and East Asian fusion food.
Rheinquai 8.
Tel: (052) 632 05 05.
www.fischerzunft.ch.
Closed: Mon & Tue.

Stein-am-Rhein

ACCOMMODATION

Rheingerbe ★★

Delightful old, wood-beamed inn. Ask for a room overlooking the River Rhine.
Schiffländi 5.
Tel: (052) 741 29 91.
www.rheingerbe.ch

Winterthur

EATING OUT

Café am Römerholz ★

Enjoy coffee and cakes, soups, salads and light snacks at this lovely

museum café overlooking beautiful gardens.
Haldenstrasse 95.
Tel: (052) 269 27 43.
www.cafeamroemerholz.ch.
Open: Tue–Sun
10am–5pm.

ENTERTAINMENT
Orchester Musikkollegium Winterthur
The renowned Musikkollegium orchestra is known for its contemporary classical repertoire.
Stadthaus.
Tel: (052) 267 67 00.
www.musikkollegium.ch

Theater Winterthur
The town's main theatre has a varied programme of plays, comedies, opera, operettas, musicals, ballet and modern dance.
Theaterstrasse 4.
Tel: (052) 267 66 80.
www.theater.winterthur.ch

Zurich
ACCOMMODATION
Hirschen ★★
A basic, family-run guesthouse at the heart of the Niederdorf district.
Niederdorfstrasse 13.
Tel: (043) 268 33 33.
www.hirschen-zuerich.ch

Leoneck ★★
This fun hotel has cow motifs throughout and rooms individually decorated by local artists in 'Swiss ethno' style.
Leonhardstrasse 1.
Tel: (044) 254 22 22.
www.leoneck.ch

Greulich ★★★
A slick boutique hotel, with minimalist furnishings and a Zen courtyard garden.
Herman-Greulich-Strasse 56. Tel: (043) 243 42 43.
www.greulich.ch

Baur au Lac ★★★★
One of Switzerland's finest traditional-style hotels set in parkland beside Lake Zurich.
Talstrasse 1.
Tel: (044) 220 50 20.
www.bauraulac.ch

Dolder Grand ★★★★
High in the hills with unrivalled views, Zurich's landmark hotel reopened in 2008, following a facelift and the addition of a state-of-the-art spa.
Kurhausstrasse 65.
Tel: (044) 456 60 00.
www.thedoldergrand.com

Widder ★★★★
Ten ancient town houses have been ingeniously interlinked to create one

of the city's top hotels, with a first-rate restaurant, rooftop terrace and modish jazz bar.
Rennweg 7.
Tel: (044) 224 25 26.
www.widderhotel.ch

EATING OUT
Adler's Swiss Confiserie Sprüngli ★
The ultimate café experience, full of old-time Zürchers enjoying Switzerland's finest cakes, chocolates and patisserie.
Bahnhofstrasse 21.
Paradeplatz. Tel: (044) 224 47 31. www.confiserie-spruengli.ch. Tram Nos: 2, 6, 7, 8, 9, 11, 13 (Paradeplatz).

Crazy Cow® ★
Try the delicious *rösti* (crispy, fried grated potato) dishes in this witty Swiss restaurant decorated with cows, Heidi, Toblerone and other local kitsch.
Leonhardstrasse 1.
Tel: (044) 261 40 55.
www.crazycow.ch.
Open: daily lunch & dinner. Tram Nos: 6, 7, 10, 15 (Haldenegg).

Lily's Stomach Supply ★
A popular Pan-Asian noodle bar with long

communal tables.
Langstrasse 197.
Tel: (044) 440 18 85.
www.lilys.ch. Open: Mon–
Thur 11am–midnight,
Fri–Sat 11am–1am, Sun
3pm–midnight. Tram
Nos: 4, 13 (Limmatplatz).

Blinde Kuh ★★

The world's first 'dark restaurant', Blinde Kuh (the German name for the game blind man's bluff) offers the unique experience of dining in total darkness. All the waiters are blind or partially sighted. Reservations recommended.
Mühlebachstrasse 148.
Tel: (044) 421 50 50.
www.blindekuh.ch. Open:
Tue–Fri 11.30am–2pm &
6–11pm, Sat–Mon
6–11pm. Tram Nos: 2, 4
(Höschgasse).

Zeughauskeller ★★

Hearty portions of Swiss fare (including 15 different types of sausage dish), washed down with fine beer.
Bahnhofstrasse 28a (Im
Gasse). Tel: (044) 211 26
90. www.zeughauskeller.ch.
Open: 11.30am–11pm.
Tram Nos: 2, 6, 7, 8, 9, 11,
13 (Paradeplatz).

Chuchi ★★★

Delicious fondues, *raclettes* (Swiss cheese dish) and local wines, served in a bright, modern, Alpine setting in the Niederdorf.
Rosengasse 10. Tel: (044)
266 96 96. www.hotel-
adler.ch. Open: 11.30am–
11.15pm. Tram Nos: 4, 15
(Rudolf-Brun-Brücke).

Tao's ★★★

Sophisticated Euro-Asian cuisine in a trendy restaurant and with a candlelit garden.
Augustinergasse 3.
Tel: 044 448 11 22.
www.taos-lounge.com.
Tram Nos: 6, 7, 11, 13
(Rennweg).

Zunfthaus zur Waag ★★★/★★★★

Enjoy classic Swiss cuisine in an elegant setting within a beautiful 17th-century guildhouse.
Münsterhof 8.
Tel: (044) 216 99 66.
www.zunfthaus-zur-
waag.ch. Tram Nos: 2, 6,
7, 8, 9, 11, 13
(Paradeplatz).

ENTERTAINMENT

Bierhalle Wolf (Bar)

There's nightly live oompah music at this authentic Germanic beer cellar in Niederdorf.
Limmatquai 132.
Tel: (044) 251 01 30.
www.bierhalle-wolf.ch.
Tram Nos: 3, 4, 6, 7, 10,
15 (Central).

Kaufleuten (Nightclub)

Mingle with stars and celebrities at Zurich's most glamorous nightclub.
Pelikanstrasse 18.
Tel: (044) 225 33 22.
www.kaufleuten.com.
Tram Nos: 6, 7, 11, 13
(Rennweg).

Moods (Jazz club)

Zurich's top jazz club.
Schiffbau, Schiffbaustrasse
6. Tel: (044) 276 80 00.
www.moods.ch.
Tram Nos: 4, 13
(Escher-Wyss-Platz).

Opernhaus (Opera)

Built in 1890 in the late baroque style, this is one of Europe's leading opera houses, famous for its world-class productions.
Falkenstrasse 1.
Tel: (044) 268 66 66.
www.opernhaus.ch. Tram
Nos: 2, 4 (Opernhaus).

Schauspielhaus (Theatre)

Switzerland's most celebrated theatre stages ground-breaking productions of classical and contemporary drama.

Zeltweg 5.
Tel: (044) 258 70 70.
www.schauspielhaus.ch.
Tram Nos: 3, 5, 8, 9
(Kunsthaus).

Schiffbau
(Club/Theatre)
An avant-garde arts complex, housed in the former red-brick 19th-century warehouse once used for building ships and lake cruisers, with a first-class restaurant, jazz club, and a venue for the Schauspielhaus (Theatre).
Schiffbaustrasse. Tram
Nos: 4, 13 (Escher-Wyss-
Platz).

Tonhalle (Classical music)
Zurich's main concert hall has an impressive and varied classical concert programme.
Claridenstrasse 7.
Tel: (044) 206 34 34.
www.tonhalle.ch. Tram
Nos: 2, 5, 8, 9, 11
(Bürkliplatz).

Tonimolkerei
(Nightclub)
Super-hip dance club in a former dairy.
Förrlibuckstrasse 109.
Tel: (044) 273 23 60.

www.tonimolkerei.com.
Tram No: 4 (Fischerweg).

SPORT AND LEISURE
Alpamare (Water park)
Europe's largest indoor water park is fun for all the family, with water slides, saunas and pools.
Gwattstrasse 12,
Pfäffikon, near Zurich.
Tel: (055) 415 15 15.
www.alpamare.ch. Open:
Tue–Thur 10am–10pm,
Fri 10am–11pm, Sat
9am–11pm, Sun & Mon
9am–10pm. Admission
charge. S-Bahn: S2, S8
(Pfäffikon).

Flussbad Obere Letten
(Lido)
Zurich's trendiest lido, on the river, with boules and beach volleyball as well as sun decks and river swimming. By night, there is a lively open-air bar with live DJs.
Lettensteg 10. Tel: (044)
362 92 00. Open: mid-
May–mid-Sept 9am–
8pm. Admission charge.
Tram Nos: 4, 13
(Limmatplatz).

Frauenbadi-
Stadthausquai (Lido)
Switzerland's last remaining 19th-century floating lido is an oasis of

calm in the city centre, open only to women for swimming and massage.
Stadthausquai. Tel: (044)
211 95 92. Open: mid-
May–mid-Sept
7.30am–7.30pm
(depending on water
temperature). Admission
charge. Tram Nos: 2, 8, 9,
11 (Börsenstrasse).

Zürirollt (Cycling)
Free bike hire from several depots around town for up to two hours at a time. You will need your passport and a small deposit per bike.
Outside the
Hauptbahnhof, Globus-
city or Operahouse.
www.zuerirollt.ch. Open:
May–Oct 8am–9.30pm
(10pm at Globus and
Opera).

NORTHWEST SWITZERLAND
Basel
ACCOMMODATION
Au Violon ★★
Once a convent, then a prison, Au Violon is now a small, stylish hotel with an excellent brasserie at the heart of the Old Town.
Im Lohnhof 4.
Tel: (061) 269 87 11.
www.au-violon.com.

Tram No: 3 (Musik Akademie).

EATING OUT

Zum Goldenen Sternen ★★★

One of Basel's oldest restaurants serving top-notch French cuisine beside the river.

St Alban-Rheinweg 70. Tel: (061) 272 16 66. www.sternen-basel.ch

ENTERTAINMENT

Stadtcasino (Classical music)

Basel's main venue for classical concerts by the Basel Symphony Orchestra and the Basel Chamber Orchestra.

Barfüsserplatz. Tel: (061) 273 73 73. www.konzerte-basel.ch, www.casinogesellschaft-basel.ch, www. kammerorchesterbasel.ch

SPORT AND LEISURE

Basler Personenschifffahrt (Boat tours)

Enjoy a city harbour tour by boat, a daytime river excursion to Rheinfelden, or an evening dinner cruise during summer months.

Tel: (061) 639 95 00. www.bpg.ch. Open: mid-Apr–mid-Oct.

Fribourg

ACCOMMODATION

Auberge aux 4 Vents ★/★★★

A characterful country house hotel, near the ice stadium, with eight rooms, each with individual décor.

Route de Grandfey 124. Tel: (026) 347 36 00. www.aux4vents.ch

EATING OUT

Café Belvédere ★★

A popular, hip locals' haunt, with delicious cocktails, international cuisine (including Japanese specialities and excellent vegetarian dishes) and a magnificent terrace overlooking the Old Town.

Grand-Rue 36. Tel: (026) 323 44 07.

Gruyères

ACCOMMODATION

Hostellerie St-Georges ★★

Charming, friendly, 16th-century building with a magnificent panoramic terrace and excellent rôtisserie-style restaurant.

Rue du Bourg 22. Tel: (026) 921 83 00. www. st-georges-gruyeres.ch

EATING OUT

Le Chalet de Gruyères ★★

Hardly surprisingly, cheese features strongly on the menu here, near the château.

Rue Principale. Tel: (026) 921 21 54. Open: 11am–10.30pm.

Neuchâtel

ACCOMMODATION

La Maison du Prussien ★★/★★★

A truly romantic hotel, in a beautifully restored ancient watermill just west of the city centre.

Rue des Tunnels 11. Tel: (032) 730 54 54. www.hotel-prussien.ch

Palafitte ★★★★

A stunning, state-of-the-art, 5-star design hotel on the banks of Lake Neuchâtel, with chic pavilions built out over the lake.

Route des Gouttes d'Or 2. Tel: (032) 723 02 02. www.palafitte.ch

EATING OUT

La Brasserie Jura ★★

A popular restaurant serving local specialities such as *fondue Neuchâteloise.*
Rue de la Treille 7.
Tel: (032) 725 14 10.
Closed: Sun.

BERNESE OBERLAND

Bern

ACCOMMODATION

Bern ★★/★★★

This smart, modern hotel is a popular choice with its chic, bright décor and friendly service.
Zeughausgasse 9.
Tel: (031) 329 22 22.
www.hotelbern.ch

EATING OUT

Kornhauskeller ★/★★

Excellent Mediterranean cuisine served in a church-like, candlelit former granary, with beautiful vaulted ceilings and frescoes.
Kornhausplatz 18.
Tel: (031) 327 72 72.
www.kornhauskeller.ch.
Open: Mon–Sat 11.45am–2.30pm & 6pm–12.30am, Sun 6–11.30pm.

Bus Nos: 3, 5, 9, 10, 12, 19, 30 (Zytglogge).

Schwellenmätteli
★★/★★★

Join the capital's smart set for trendy fusion cuisine and sensational brunch buffets in the rustic 'casa' or on the cutting-edge floating 'Terrasse' on the River Aare.
Dalmaziquai 11.
Tel: (031) 350 50 01.
www.schwellenmaetteli.ch.
Open: Tue 11.45am–2.30pm & 6pm–midnight, Wed–Fri 11.45am–2.30pm, Sat 6pm–midnight, Sun 11.45am–midnight. Closed: Mon.

ENTERTAINMENT

Bern Symphony Orchestra

One of Switzerland's finest symphony orchestras, staging concerts at the Casino, the Münster and the Stadttheater.
Stiftung Berner Symphonie-Orchester, Münzgraben 2.
Tel: (031) 328 24 24.
www.bsorchester.ch

Berner Puppentheater

Puppet theatre for young and old, in a former wine cellar.

Gerechtigkeitsgasse 31.
Tel: (031) 311 95 85.
www.berner-puppentheater.ch.
Bus No: 12.

Marian's Jazzroom

One of the nation's best jazz clubs.
Hotel Innere Enge, Engestrasse 54.
Tel: (031) 309 61 11.
www.mariansjazzroom.ch.
Open: Sept–May Tue–Sat (2 concerts nightly at 7.30pm & 10pm). Bus No: 21 (Bremgarten).

Narrenpacktheater

Specialises in lively folk theatre.
Kramgasse 30.
Tel: (031) 352 05 17.
www.narrenpack.ch

Stadttheater Bern

Bern's most beautiful theatre and the primary venue for the resident opera company and contemporary dance troupe.
Kornhausplatz 20.
Tel: (031) 329 52 52.
www.stadttheaterbern.ch

SPORT AND LEISURE

Stade de Suisse

Switzerland's largest sports stadium has capacity for 36,000 spectators.

Nationalstadion,
Papiermühlestrasse 71,
Wankdorf.
Tel: (031) 344 88 88.
www.stadedesuisse.ch

Eigergletscher
ACCOMMODATION
Guesthouse
Eigergletscher ★
The highest guesthouse
on the Jungfrau rail
route, it was constructed
in 1898 to accommodate
the railway builders, and
is today popular with
hikers and skiers.
Bahnhof Eigergletscher.
Tel: (033) 828 78 66.

Grindelwald
ACCOMMODATION
Gletschergarten ★★
This beautiful, flower-
festooned chalet-hotel
oozes rustic charm
but has modern
amenities.
Tel: (033) 853 17 21.
www.hotel-
gletschergarten.ch

EATING OUT
Onkel Tom's Hütte ★
Delicious wood-fired
pizzas and salads served
in a cosy wooden hut.
Im Graben 4.
Tel: (033) 853 52 39.

Open: Tue 4–10.30pm,
Wed–Sun noon–2pm &
4pm–midnight.

Gstaad
ACCOMMODATION
Posthotel Rössli ★★/★★★
A small, family-run,
3-star hotel at the heart of
Gstaad's pedestrian zone,
with cosy, comfortable
pine-clad bedrooms and
traditional mountain
cuisine in the restaurant.
Promenade.
Tel: (033) 748 42 42.
www.posthotelroessli.ch
Palace Hotel
Gstaad ★★★★
This landmark hotel, with
its neo-medieval façade is
a legendary hideaway for
the rich and famous.
Palacestrasse. Tel: (033)
748 50 00. www.palace.ch

EATING OUT
Chesery ★★★★
This is one of
Switzerland's top eateries,
and *the* place to rub
shoulders with the rich
and famous. Reservations
are essential.
Lauenenstrasse.
Tel: (033) 744 24 51.
www.chesery.ch. Closed:
mid-Apr–mid-June &
mid-Oct–mid-Dec.

Interlaken
ACCOMMODATION
Alphorn ★/★★
This homely, old-
fashioned B&B is within
walking distance of the
town centre and is a
popular family option.
Rothornstrasse 29A.
Tel: (033) 822 30 51.
www.hotel-alphorn.ch
Victoria-Jungfrau Grand
Hotel & Spa ★★★★
This grand Victorian
building was
headquarters for the
Swiss Army during World
War II. Today, it contains
Interlaken's top hotel,
with beautiful gardens
and a sumptuous spa.
Höheweg 41.
Tel: (033) 828 28 28.
www.victoria-jungfrau.ch

EATING OUT
Hirschen ★★
Hearty schnitzels, ragouts,
fondues and other
nourishing Swiss
staples are the speciality
at this old wooden-
beamed inn.
Hauptstrasse 11, Matten.
Tel: (033) 822 15 45. www.
hirschen-interlaken.ch.
Open: Tue–Sat 11am–
1.30pm, 4.30–11pm,
Sun 9am–10pm.

ENTERTAINMENT

Tell Freilichtspiele (Tell Open-Air Theatre)

Friedrich Schiller's celebrated *William Tell* story has been staged in the Rugen Woods near Interlaken every summer since 1912.

Tellbüro, Höheweg 37, Interlaken. Tel: (033) 822 37 22. www.tellspiele.ch. Open: late June–early Sept.

Kleine Scheidegg

ACCOMMODATION

Hôtel Bellevue des Alpes ★★★/★★★★

This traditional hotel at the foot of the Eiger is a veritable oasis of peace, high in the mountains.

Tel: (033) 855 12 12. www.scheidegg-hotels.ch

Lauterbrunnen

ACCOMMODATION

Camping Jungfrau ★

A superb family-run campsite, situated in the 'valley of 72 waterfalls' near the famous Staubbach Falls, and the skiing areas of Wengen and Mürren.

Tel: (033) 856 20 10. www.camping-jungfrau.ch

Mürren

ACCOMMODATION

Alpenruh ★

This attractive, chalet-style hotel is located beside the Schilthorn cable car. Ask for a room with a view of the Jungfrau.

Tel: (033) 856 88 00. www. alpenruh-muerren.ch

Wengen

ACCOMMODATION

Bären ★

A charming chalet hotel with a relaxed atmosphere and an excellent restaurant.

Tel: (033) 855 14 19. www.baeren-wengen.ch

EATING OUT

Mary's Café ★

Located near the Lauberhorn downhill race course, serving hearty mountain fare and delicious alcoholic coffees.

Staubbachbänkli, Schiltwald. Tel: (033) 855 25 26.

LAKE GENEVA REGION

Château-d'Oex

ACCOMMODATION

Hostellerie Bon Accueil ★★

This authentic, 18th-century chalet, with beautiful wood-panelled rooms and traditional country-style furnishings, makes an ideal base for walkers and skiers.

La Frasse. Tel: (026) 924 63 20. www.bonaccueil.ch

Chexbres

ENTERTAINMENT

Le Deck (Bar)

A chic, open-air lounge bar overhanging the Lavaux vineyards with deep sofas and sensational lake vistas.

Hotel Restaurant Le Baron Tavernier, route de la Corniche Tel: (021) 926 60 00. www.barontavernier.com. Open: Apr–Oct 11am–midnight.

Les Diablerets

EATING OUT

Restaurant Botta 3000 ★★

This ultramodern, cuboid restaurant, designed by Mario Botta atop the glacier, affords great views of the Alps.

Tel: (024) 492 09 31. www.glacier3000.ch. Open: 9am–4.30pm.

Epesses

ENTERTAINMENT

Caveau des Vignerons d'Epesses (Wine cellar)

One of several wine-tasting cellars showcasing the local Lavaux wines.
Grand-Rue. Tel: (079) 378 42 49. www.caveau-epesses.ch. Open: mid-Apr–June Fri–Sun 5–9pm; July–early Oct 5–9pm.

Geneva

ACCOMMODATION

Tiffany ★★★

An Art Nouveau boutique hotel in the heart of the cultural and arts district.
Rue de l'Arquebuse 20. Tel: (022) 708 16 16. www.hotel-tiffany.ch

Beau-Rivage ★★★★

Housed in a magnificent Belle Époque mansion facing the lake, this 5-star hotel is the epitome of luxury and elegance.
Quai du Mont-Blanc 13. Tel: (022) 716 66 66. www.beau-rivage.ch. Bus No: 1 (Monthoux).

EATING OUT

Brasserie du Bourg-de-Four ★★

This tiny Art Nouveau-style brasserie is popular with local Genevois for its delicious steaks, salads, tartares and *rösti* dishes.
Place du Bourg-du-Four 13. Tel: (022) 311 90 76. Closed: Sun evenings.

Chez Jacky ★★/★★★

This small, simple bistro near the train station specialises in seafood and serves beautifully prepared international cuisine with an imaginative twist. Booking is essential.
Rue Necker 9–11. Tel: (022) 732 86 80. www.chezjacky.ch. Open: Mon–Fri 11.30am–2pm & 7–10pm. Closed: Sat, Sun & Aug.

ENTERTAINMENT

b-club

A sophisticated, cosmopolitan crowd frequents this lively nightclub beneath trendy Café Baroque.
Place de la Fusterie 12. Tel: (022) 311 05 15. www.lebaroque.com. Open: Mon–Sat 11pm–5am.

Grand Théâtre de Genève

The opera and ballet season runs from September until July.
Place Neuve. Tel: (022) 418 31 30. www.geneveopera.ch

Victoria Hall (Classical music)

Geneva's most celebrated classical musical venue and home of the Orchestra de la Suisse Romande.
Rue du Général Dufour 14. Tel: (022) 418 35 13. www.osr.ch

SPORT AND LEISURE

Genève-Plage (Lido)

Geneva's summer lido is fun for all the family with its swimming pools, water slides, sun decks, beach volleyball and boules.
Port-Noir, Cologny. Tel: (022) 736 24 82. www.geneve-plage.ch. Open: late May–mid-Sept 10am–8pm. Admission charge.

Société Nautique de Genève (Nautical Club)

Sailing boats for hire; arranges courses in sailing, waterskiing and wakeboarding during summer months.
Port-Noir, Cologny. Tel: (022) 707 05 00. www.nautique.org

Lausanne
ACCOMMODATION
Aulac ★★
A comfortable 3-star hotel by the lake in Ouchy, near the Olympic Museum. Ask for a room overlooking the lake.
Place de la Navigation 4.
Tel: (021) 613 15 00.
www.aulac.ch

EATING OUT
Café Romand ★/★★
This ancient brasserie is a Lausanne institution, specialising in traditional dishes from the Vaud region.
Place St-François 2.
Tel: (021) 312 63 75.
www.caferomand.com.
Open: 11am–11pm.

ENTERTAINMENT
Béjart Ballet Lausanne
Book early for performances by this world-famous dance academy.
Chemin du Presbytère.
Tel: (021) 641 64 80.
www.bejart.ch
Mad (Moulin à Danses) (Nightclub)
Lausanne's best-known dance club, with five floors attracting the world's top DJs.

Rue de Genève 23.
Tel: (021) 340 69 69.
www.mad.ch
Théâtre de Vidy
This theatre is renowned throughout Europe for its innovative productions.
Avenue Émile-Jacques Dalcroze 5. Tel: (021) 619 45 45. www.vidy.ch

Leysin
ACCOMMODATION
Le Grand Chalet ★★
This 3-star family-run chalet is conveniently located, near the train station and ski lifts.
Tel: (024) 493 01 01.
www.grand-chalet.ch

EATING OUT
Kuklos ★★
One of only three revolving mountain restaurants in the world, sleek Kuklos affords an exceptional 360-degree Alpine panorama.
Tel: (024) 494 31 41.
www.teleleysin.ch

SPORT AND LEISURE
Tobogganing Park
The only toboggan park in Switzerland where you can go snow-tubing down carved-out pistes similar to bobsleigh runs.

Tel: (024) 494 28 88.
www.tobogganing.ch.
Open: Dec–Mar Mon 2–6pm, Tue–Sun 10am–6pm.

Lutry
EATING OUT
Café de la Poste ★/★★
This tiny lakeside restaurant is *the* place to eat perch fillets fresh from the lake.
48 Grand Rue.
Tel: (021) 791 18 72.
Closed: Sun & Mon.

Montreux
ACCOMMODATION
Fairmont Le Montreux Palace ★★★/★★★★
This Belle Époque extravaganza by the lake counts among the Swiss Riviera's top hotels, with an impressive spa.
Grand-Rue 100.
Tel: (021) 962 12 12.
www.montreux-palace.com

EATING OUT
La Rouvenaz ★/★★
An Italian restaurant near the lakefront that specialises in seafood.
Rue du Marché 1.
Tel: (021) 963 27 36.

www.montreux.ch/
rouvenaz-hotel

Le Palais Oriental

★★/★★★

This exquisite Moorish-style restaurant serves a varied menu of Iranian, Lebanese and Moroccan cuisine.

Quai Ernest Ansermet 6.
Tel: (021) 963 12 71.
www.palaisoriental.ch.
Closed: 24 Dec–Jan.

Le Pont de Brent ★★★★

Le Pont de Brent is one of the nation's top restaurants, serving Gérard Rabaey's outstanding 3-Michelin-starred haute cuisine in surroundings of understated elegance.

Brent-Montreux.
Tel: (021) 964 52 30.
www.lepontdebrent.com.
Closed: Sun & Mon.

ENTERTAINMENT

Casino Barrière de Montreux

This glitzy lakeside casino is one of the main venues for the celebrated Jazz Festival (*see p19*). Passports are required for entry.

Rue du Théâtre 9. Tel:
(021) 962 83 83. www.
casinodemontreux.ch.

Open: Sun–Thur 11am–3am, Fri & Sat 11am–5am.

Le Piano Bar

A stylish cocktail bar, with dazzling views of Lake Geneva and an impressive wine list featuring over 70 varieties of champagne.

Hotel Le Mirador
Kempinski, Mont-Pélerin.
Tel: (021) 925 11 11.
www.mirador.ch

Montreux Music & Convention Centre

This massive complex is one of the main venues for the Montreux International Jazz Festival (*see p19*) and other arts events.

Quai de Vernex.
Tel: (021) 962 20 00.
www.montreuxcongres.ch

Vevey

ACCOMMODATION

Camping de la Pichette ★

A small, tranquil campsite beside a tiny harbour on the banks of Lake Geneva.

Chemin de la Paix 37, Corseaux.
Tel: (021) 921 09 97.

Riviera Lodge ★

A simple backpackers' hostel near the lake and the train station in a

19th-century town house.

Place du Marché 5.
Tel: (021) 923 80 40.
www.rivieralodge.ch

Des Trois Couronnes ★★★★

This palatial spa hotel by the lake combines tradition with state-of-the-art amenities.

Rue d'Italie 49.
Tel: (021) 923 32 00.
www.hoteltroiscouronnes.ch

EATING OUT

Le Mazot ★★

Enjoy juicy horse steaks, fondues and regional fish dishes in a rustic setting in the Old Town.

Rue du Conseil 7.
Tel: (021) 921 78 22.
Open: 11am– 2pm &
6pm–midnight. Closed:
Wed & Sun lunch.

Villars-sur-Ollon

SPORT AND LEISURE

Golf Club Villars

Each of the 18 holes has magnificent Alpine panoramas, including Mont Blanc and the Dents du Midi.

Route du Col de la Croix.
Tel: (024) 495 42 14.
www.golf-villars.ch.
Open: May–Oct.

VALAIS
Champéry
(Portes du Soleil)
ACCOMMODATION
Beau-Séjour ★★
A beautiful chalet hotel
facing the Dents du
Midi, and with easy
access to the ski lifts.
Rue du Village 114.
Tel: (024) 479 58 58.
www.beausejour-
champery.com

Champoussin
EATING OUT
Chez Gaby ★/★★
A traditional Alpine
restaurant serving
delicious mountain
cuisine in a cosy setting
overlooking the Dents
du Midi.
Tel: (024) 477 22 22.
www.chezgaby.ch

Crans-Montana
ACCOMMODATION
Du Lac ★
A small, friendly chalet
hotel on the shore of
Lake Grenon, with 30
simple, modern
bedrooms, internet
café and mountain-
bike hire.
Tel: (027) 481 34 14.
www.hoteldulac-crans-
montana.ch

Grand Hôtel du
Golf ★★★/★★★★
This 5-star landmark
hotel built in 1907 has
been run by the same
family since World
War I.
Tel: (027) 485 42 42.
www.grand-hotel-du-
golf.ch

SPORT AND LEISURE
Golf Club Crans-sur-
Sierre
Of its four courses, the
famous 18-hole circuit
named after its designer,
Severiano Ballesteros, is
one of the most beautiful
courses in the world, and
the venue of the annual
European Masters
Tournament.
Tel: (027) 485 97 97.
www.golfcrans.ch

Grimentz
EATING OUT
Becs-de-Bosson ★★
This simple, rustic hotel-
restaurant serves delicious
Valaisan fare including
Annivard onion soup
with cheese and rye
bread, traditional raclette
(Swiss cheese dish), and
delicious game.
Tel: (027) 475 19 79.
www.becsdebosson.ch

Les Cerniers
ACCOMMODATION
Whitepod ★★★/★★★★
At the foot of the Dents
du Midi, award-winning,
eco-friendly white tents
(or 'pods') offer the
ultimate mountain
retreat for the
environmentally
conscious.
Les Cerniers, Les Giettes
(near Martigny).
Tel: (024) 471 38 38.
www.whitepod.com

Leukerbad
SPORT AND LEISURE
Burgerbad Thermal
Centre/Lindner
Alpentherme
Leukerbad is the largest
spa and wellness resort in
the Alps, and the highest
in Europe at 1,411m,
(4,629ft), with 3.9 million
litres (858,000 gallons)
of thermal water.
Burgerbad. Tel: (027) 472
20 20. www.burgerbad.ch.
Lindner Alpentherme.
Tel: (027) 472 10 00.
www.alpentherme.ch

Moiry
ACCOMMODATION
Cabane de Moiry ★
There's a jolly, communal
atmosphere at this small,

simple mountain retreat beside the Zinal glacier.
Tel: (024) 494 19 34 (winter); (027) 475 45 34 (summer). www.cabane-de-moiry.ch

Saas Fee
EATING OUT
Fletschhorn ★★★★
One of Switzerland's top restaurants, serving the exquisite Alpine cuisine of one of Switzerland's top chefs, Markus Neff.
Tel: (027) 957 21 31. www.fletschhorn.ch. Closed: mid-Apr–mid-June & late Oct–mid-Dec.

ENTERTAINMENT
Nesti's Ski Bar
Head straight from the pistes to this riotous bar for early-evening après-ski.
Tel: (027) 957 21 12.

Sierre
EATING OUT
Didier de Courten ★★★★
The sensational fusion cuisine of this elegant 2-Michelin-starred restaurant is a veritable feast for the senses. Reservations recommended.

Rue du Bourg 1. Tel: (027) 455 13 51. www.hotel-terminus.ch. Closed: Sun & Mon.

St-Jean
EATING OUT
La Gougra ★★
This small, rustic, family-run restaurant serves mouth-watering Valaisan cuisine, and one of the best fondues in Valais.
Tel: (027) 475 13 03. www.lagougra.ch. Closed: Thur.

St-Luc
ACCOMMODATION
Bella-Tola ★★/★★★
The plain shuttered façade of this historic hotel belies an elegant, traditional interior, with luxurious bedrooms, beautiful spa facilities, log fires and two excellent restaurants.
Tel: (027) 475 14 44. www.bellatola.ch

Verbier
ACCOMMODATION
The Bunker ★
Cheap, basic underground dormitory accommodation in a converted atomic bomb shelter and mid-range

accommodation in the Summer House, plus free use of the swimming pools and ice rink at the neighbouring sports centre.
Centre Sportif. Tel: (027) 771 66 01. www.thebunker.ch
Chalet d'Adrian ★★★★
Verbier's top hotel, by the Savoleyres ski lift, has just 25 rooms, excellent cuisine and a spa.
Chemin des Creux. Tel: (027) 771 62 00. www.chalet-adrien.com. Closed: May, June, Oct & Nov.
The Lodge Verbier ★★★★
Richard Branson's latest enterprise, this luxurious nine-bedroom chalet is hidden in the woods just off one of the ski runs, and offers unadulterated luxury, with an indoor heated pool, whirlpool, Virgin Touch spa and mini ice rink.
Chemin de Plénadzeu 3. Tel: +44(0) 208 600 0430 (UK booking office). www.verbierlodge.ch

EATING OUT
Cabane de Montfort ★
Of Verbier's 37 mountain restaurants, this is one of the best sited, serving

soups, sandwiches and hearty regional fare to hungry skiers on a suntrap terrace beneath Montfort. There is also some simple accommodation.
Tel: (027) 778 13 84.
www.cabanemontfort.ch.
Open: Dec–mid-May, end June–Sept.

Le Bouchon Gourmand ★★
A lovely, atmospheric French bistro, specialising in foie gras, duck dishes, salads and pastas.
Rue de la Poste.
Tel: (027) 771 72 96.

ENTERTAINMENT
Farm Club (Nightclub)
Despite its extortionate prices, The Farm remains Verbier's leading nightclub, and the place to hang out in the Alps.
Tel: (027) 771 61 21.
www.farmclub.ch.
Open: 11pm–4am.

Pub Mont Fort
Happy hour (*Jan–Apr 4–5pm*) is especially popular with Brits and chalet girls at this Verbier institution. It also gets lively later in the evening.
Chemin de la Tinte 10.
Tel: (027) 771 48 98.

www.pubmontfort.com.
Open: Nov–Apr, mid-June–Aug 3pm–1.30am.

SPORT AND LEISURE
Warren Smith Ski Academy
A ski school with a difference, focusing on freeride and powder skiing, steep terrain, freestyle and heli-skiing.
Chalet Zapreskie Point, Chemin d'Amon 22.
Tel: +44(0) 1525 374757.
www.warrensmith-skiacademy.com

Zermatt
ACCOMMODATION
Berghaus Matterhorn ★★
The start point for climbing the Matterhorn, this traditional mountain chalet offers dormitory-style accommodation and a hearty evening meal.
Tel: (027) 967 22 64.
www.berghaus-matterhorn.ch

Riffelalp Resort 2222m ★★★★
With spectacular views of the Matterhorn, this top-notch, ski-in, ski-out hotel boasts a beautiful spa and Europe's highest outdoor pool.

Tel: (027) 699 05 55.
www.riffelalp.com

EATING OUT
Stockhorn Grill ★★
Delicious Swiss fare, including meat grilled over a wood fire, in a popular restaurant owned by the family of legendary Matterhorn guide Emil Julen.
Riedstrasse. Tel: (027) 967 17 47. www.grill-stockhorn.ch. Open: mid-June–early Oct & mid-Nov–early May.

ENTERTAINMENT
Hennu Stall (Bar)
This small open-air après-ski hut, on the ski slope above the resort, serves schnapps, Irish coffees, vodka shots and other heart-warming drinks.
Tel: (079) 213 36 69.
www.hennustall.ch

Papperla Pub
This is the best après-ski pub, with a wild party atmosphere, DJ and dancing. When the evening progresses, move next door to the Schneewittchen nightclub.
Steinmattenstrasse 34.
Tel: (027) 967 40 40.
www.papperlapub.ch.

Open: 2.30pm–2am (club is open until 4am).

SPORT AND LEISURE
Alpin Center Zermatt
This company specialises in extreme Alpine sports, including mountaineering, heli-skiing, and high-altitude climbing tours.
Tel (027) 966 24 60.
www.alpincenter-zermatt.ch

CENTRAL SWITZERLAND
Andermatt
ACCOMMODATION
Drei Könige ★★
A traditional-style hotel near the village centre, with a sauna, whirlpool and eucalyptus steam bath to soothe the aching muscles of skiers and trekkers.
Gotthardstrasse 69.
Tel: (041) 887 00 01.
www.3koenige.ch

Engelberg
ACCOMMODATION
Bellevue-Terminus ★
Don't be put off by the faded appearance of this Victorian hotel. It is one of Switzerland's popular backpacker hotels, and offers excellent value for money.
Bahnhofplatz.
Tel: (041) 639 68 68.
www.bellevue-engelberg.ch

SPORT AND LEISURE
Swiss Ski School Engelberg-Titlis
One of a nationwide group of Swiss ski schools providing world-class ski and snowboard instruction.
Tourist Center.
Tel: (041) 639 54 54 (skiing and snowboarding), (041) 639 54 50 (adventure sports).
www.skischule-engelberg.ch

Luzern
ACCOMMODATION
Backpackers Lucerne ★
This superb hostel beside the lake is extremely popular, with clean, bright family rooms, and bikes and rollerblades for hire.
Alpenquai 42.
Tel: (041) 360 04 20.
www.backpackerslucerne.ch

Magic ★★/★★★
A wonderfully eccentric hotel in the medieval district, with themed bedrooms. Choose from Swiss chalet, Aladdin or pirate décor.
Kornmarkt. Tel: (041) 417 12 20. www.magic-hotel.ch

Montana ★★★
Overlooking Luzern, the lake and Mount Pilatus, this magnificent 4-star Art Deco hotel is accessed by its own funicular. There is also a beautiful rooftop sun terrace, and weekly jazz in the hotel bar.
Adligenswilerstrasse 22.
Tel: (041) 419 00 00.
www.hotel-montana.ch

The Hotel ★★★/★★★★
French designer Jean Nouvel (*see p57*) has cleverly converted this old town house into an ultra-modern boutique hotel, with minimalist décor.
Sempacherstrasse 14.
Tel: (041) 226 86 86.
www.the-hotel.ch

EATING OUT
Schützengarten ★
The simple, tiled floor and wooden tables provide a perfect backdrop for unfussy but delicious vegetarian cuisine.
Bruchstrasse 20.
Tel: (041) 240 01 10. www.schuetzengartenluzern.ch.

*Open: Mon–Sat
9am–11pm.*
Jasper ★★★/★★★★
One of Luzern's top
eateries, serving
innovative Swiss cuisine
in an avant-garde setting
with dazzling lake views.
*Haldenstrasse 10. Tel:
(041) 416 16 16. www.
palace-luzern.com. Open:
noon–2pm & 7–10pm.*

ENTERTAINMENT
**Kultur- und
Kongresszentrum
Luzern (Lucerne Culture
and Conference Centre)**
The futuristic KKL
building, designed by
French architect Nouvel
(*see p57*), contains a
concert hall with near-
perfect acoustics and is
the venue of Luzern's
celebrated International
Festival of Music
(*see p19*).
*Europaplatz 1.
Tel: (041) 226 70 70.
www.kkl-luzern.ch.
Open: 11pm–4am.
Closed: Sun–Tue.*
Pravda (Nightclub)
The trendiest dance club
in town attracts an
impressive list of
visiting Swiss and
international DJs.

*Pilatusstrasse 29. Tel:
(041) 226 88 88. www.
pravda.ch. Open: 11pm–
4am. Closed: Sun–Tue.*

Pilatus
ACCOMMODATION
Hotel Pilatus Kulm ★
Enjoy the romantic starry
night and the sensational
sunrise at this simple,
traditional-style hotel
on the summit of
Mount Pilatus.
*Schlossweg 1, Kriens.
Tel: (041) 329 12 12.
www.pilatus.ch*

Schwyz
ACCOMMODATION
Hotel Wysses Rössli ★★
A popular 4-star hotel in
the main square, with
large, bright rooms and
an excellent restaurant.
*Hauptplatz 3.
Tel: (041) 811 19 22.
www.roessli-schwyz.ch*

EATING OUT
Wysses Rössli ★★
This classic Swiss dining
room oozes tradition and
quality, with its excellent
choice of regional fare.
*Hauptplatz 3.
Tel: (041) 811 19 22.
www.roessli-schwyz.ch.
Open: 7pm–midnight.*

Zug
ACCOMMODATION
Löwen am See ★★★
An attractive hotel with
spacious, modern rooms
overlooking the Zugersee
(Lake Zuger). It has a
popular Mediterranean
restaurant.
*Landsgemeinderplatz.
Tel: (041) 725 22 22.
www.loewen-zug.ch*

EATING OUT
**Confiserie Albert
Meier ★**
Try the local speciality,
Zuger Kirschtorte, a
scrumptious almond
cake saturated with
kirsch (cherry brandy).
*Alpenstrasse 16.
Tel: (041) 711 10 49.
www.diezugerkirschtorte.ch.
Open: Mon–Fri
7am–6.30pm, Sat
8am–4pm. Closed: Sun.*

EASTERN
SWITZERLAND
Arosa
ACCOMMODATION
Alpina ★
A chalet-style hotel near
the town centre with
plenty of traditional
charm.
*Tel: (081) 377 16 58.
www.alpina-arosa.ch.*

Closed: mid-Apr–mid-June & mid-Oct–mid-Dec.

Eating out
Alpenblick ★★
This mountain restaurant on the slopes serves hearty meat dishes, fondues, home-made strudels and their speciality, *Schümli Pflümli* – coffee with plum liqueur and cream.
Tel: (081) 377 14 28.
www.alpenblick-arosa.ch.
Open: Dec–mid-Apr 9am–11.30pm.

Chur
Sport and Leisure
Swissraft
One of a number of nationwide Swissraft bases, this company offers rafting, canyoning, ballooning, mountain biking, paragliding and other adventure sports.
Punt Arsa, Dornat/Ems (near Chur).
Tel: (081) 911 52 50.
www.swissraft.ch

Davos
Accommodation
Larix ★★
In a resort of mostly large, deluxe hotels, this traditional-style hotel is a real find, with attractive, individually designed rooms, sauna and steam room at an affordable price.
Obere Albertistrasse 10, Davos-Platz.
Tel: (081) 413 11 88.
www.hotel-larix.ch
Iglu-Dorf ★★/★★★
The 'Igloo Village' at Davos-Klosters converts a simple overnight stay into an unforgettable snowy adventure, with its cosy sheepskins and expedition sleeping bags (*see p129*).
Tel: (041) 612 27 28.
www.iglu-dorf.com.
Open: 25 Dec–mid-Apr.

Eating out
Gentiana ★★
A busy Alpine bistro, best known for its ten different types of fondue and a surprising variety of snail dishes. Wine is served by the carafe and there are some delicious desserts. Booking recommended.
Promenade 53, Davos-Platz. Tel: (081) 413 56 49. Open: 11am–2.30pm & 6–11pm (winter),
11am–11pm (summer).
Closed: Wed in summer.

Klosters
Accommodation
Jugendherberge Klosters (Youth Hostel Klosters) ★
A popular choice with families, this friendly hostel offers simple but cosy accommodation.
Soldanella, Talstrasse 73.
Tel: (081) 422 13 16.
www.youthhostel.ch/ klosters

Laax
Accommodation
Riders Palace ★
A trendy, design hotel with high-tech bedrooms and bathrooms by Philippe Starck, some dormitory-style accommodation, a lively après-ski bar and occasional live bands.
Laax Murschetg.
Tel: (081) 927 97 00.
www.riderspalace.ch

Scuol
Accommodation
Hotel Engiadina ★★
This delightful boutique hotel has stylish, traditional décor and an excellent candlelit restaurant.

Tel: (081) 864 14 21.
www.hotel-engiadina.ch

EATING OUT
Traube ★★
This simple restaurant is excellent value for money, with friendly service, tasty traditional Swiss dishes and a cosy atmosphere.
Hotel Traube, Via Stradun. Tel: (081) 861 07 00. www.traube.ch.
Open: Mon, Thur–Sun noon–11pm; Tue–Wed 6–11pm.
Closed: Nov & May.

St Moritz
ACCOMMODATION
Badrutt's Palace ★★★★
One of the world's most famous winter sports hotels offering the very best of Swiss hospitality.
Via Serlas 27.
Tel: (081) 837 10 00.
www.badruttspalace.com.
Open: early Dec–mid-Apr & mid-June–mid-Sept.

EATING OUT
Hanselmann ★
An olde-worlde coffee house, located at the heart of St Moritz overlooking the lake, and reputedly serving the best cakes in the Alps.

Via Maistra 8. Tel: (081) 833 38 64.
www.hanselmann.ch
Post Haus ★★★
This sleek new restaurant-cum-lounge-bar, specialising in delicious grills and Contemporary Alpine Gastrosophy®, is the first restaurant designed by British architect, Lord Norman Foster, and his second project in St Moritz.
Via dal Vout 3.
Tel: (081) 833 80 80.
www.post-haus.ch.
Restaurant open: 11.30am–midnight.
Lounge open: 3pm–2am.
Closed: May, mid-June–Oct (Sun & Mon) & Nov.
Jöhri's Talvo ★★★★
The restaurant of Roland Jöhri, the region's best chef with two Michelin stars for his inventive Swiss cuisine, is housed within a beautiful 17th-century Engadine house 3.2km (2 miles) south of St Moritz.
Via Gunels 15, Champfèr.
Tel: (081) 833 44 55.
www.talvo.ch.
Closed: Mon & Tue (summer); Mon & Tue lunchtime (winter); late

Sept–early Dec & mid-Apr–late June.
La Marmite – Mathis Food Affairs ★★★★
High upon the slopes of the Corviglia ski area at 2,486m (8,156ft), this esteemed restaurant serves haute cuisine with caviar and truffle-rich dishes – living up to its reputation as the best (and most expensive) high-altitude lunch experience in the Alps.
Tel: (081) 833 63 55.
www.mathisfood.ch

ENTERTAINMENT
Devil's Place (Bar)
This bar is in the *Guinness Book of Records* for having the world's largest range of malt whisky.
Hotel Waldhaus am See, Via Dim Lej.
Tel: (081) 836 60 00.
www.waldhaus-am-see.ch.
Open: 4pm–12.30am.
King's Club
Rub shoulders with the rich and famous at this Moroccan-themed disco – the top nightspot in St Moritz.
Badrutt's Palace, via Serlas 27.
Tel: (081) 837 10 00.

Sport and leisure

Cresta Run

Surely the ultimate adrenalin rush. The Cresta Run has been a sport here since 1885, with riders (men only) lying head-first on metal toboggans, speeding down an ice track to Celerina at up to 130kph (80mph). You will need temporary membership.

www.cresta-run.com

Olympic Bob Run

Since the world's only natural ice bob run opened at Celerina in 1890, the St Moritz Bobsleigh Club has hosted over 30 world championships. The two- and four-man bob championships draw huge crowds for the training as well as the races.

Tel: (081) 830 02 00.
www.olympia-bobrun.ch.
Open: Christmas–end Feb.

Schweizer Langlaufschule St Moritz (Swiss Cross-Country Ski School)

Friendly classes, professional instruction (by former Olympic medallist and Swiss champion Albert Giger and his team) and a beautiful setting make cross-country skiing enjoyable and fun.

Langlaufzentrum, Plazza Paracelsus 2.
Tel: (081) 833 62 33.

Snow Golf

Try your hand at snow golf. The greens are called 'whites', the balls are orange, the holes are bigger, the putting surfaces are like marble, and the bunkers are full of snow.

Tel: (081) 838 60 00 for further details.

'Snow Night'

Every Friday at 7pm during the ski season, it's party time on the slopes below Corvatsch Mittelstation, with the longest illuminated piste in Switzerland followed by the liveliest après-ski of the week.

Snow Polo

Each January, celebrities, royals and aristocrats gather to watch the 'sport of kings' at the annual Snow Polo championships on the frozen lake at St Moritz – it is undoubtedly the social event of the season.

www.polostmoritz.com

White Turf St Moritz

It's hard to beat the spectacle of hooves thundering through clouds of snow spray in the world's only *skikjöring* competitions, with men on skis pulled along by unmounted thoroughbreds.

Tel: (081) 833 84 60.
www.whiteturf.ch

TICINO

Ascona

Accommodation

Hotel Giardino ★★★★

A glamorous, extravagant spa retreat in the midst of beautiful gardens, with romantic rooms and a gourmet restaurant.

Via Segnale 10.
Tel: (091) 785 88 88.
www.giardino.ch

Entertainment

Settimane Musicali (Classical music)

From the end of August to mid-October, the resort resounds to classical music concerts in its celebrated Settimane Musicali, which draws the world's top artistes and orchestras.

Tel: (091) 785 19 65.
www.settimane-musicali.ch

Bellinzona

EATING OUT

Malakoff ★★

Try the delicious home-made pasta and some of the many types of Ticinese Alpine cheese in this friendly *trattoria.*
Via Bacilieri 10, Bellinzona-Ravecchia.
Tel: (091) 825 49 40.
Open: Mon–Sat 12–2pm & 7–10pm. Closed: Aug & 1–15 Jan.

Locanda Orico ★★/★★★

Chef Lorenzo Albrici is famed for his creative cuisine at this highly regarded gourmet restaurant.
Via Orico 13.
Tel: (091) 825 15 18.
www.locandaorico.ch.
Closed: Sun & Mon & mid-July–mid-Aug.

ENTERTAINMENT

Teatro Sociale Bellinzona (Theatre)

Built 150 years ago in the style of Milan's celebrated La Scala opera house, this is Switzerland's finest example of classic theatre architecture.
Piazza Teatro.
Tel: (091) 825 48 18.
www.teatrosociale.ch

Locarno

ACCOMMODATION

Cittadella ★★

This friendly hotel offers ten simple, Italianate-style rooms above a popular fish restaurant.
Via Cittadella 18.
Tel: (091) 751 58 85.
www.cittadella.ch

EATING OUT

Osteria Chiara ★★/★★★

This authentic grotto restaurant draws locals and visitors for its cosy ambience and southern Italian cuisine.
Vicolo dei Chiara 1, Muralto.
Tel: (091) 743 32 96.
www.osteriachiara.ch.
Open: Tue–Sat 9am–2pm & 7pm–midnight.
Closed: Sun & Mon.

ENTERTAINMENT

Festival Internazionale del Film

Every August for ten days, the main square of Piazza Grande is converted into Europe's largest open-air cinema and shows 'auteur' films.
Piazza Grande.
Tel: (091) 756 21 21.
www.pardo.ch

Lugano

ACCOMMODATION

The Oasis Youth Hostel ★

Housed in the attractive Villa Savosa, this popular hostel is excellent value.
Via Cantonale 13, Savosa.
Tel: (091) 966 27 28.
www.luganoyouthhostel.ch.
Open: Mar–Nov.

EATING OUT

La Tinera ★

Tuck into tasty Ticinese cuisine at this popular grotto-style restaurant. Try the risotto or polenta dishes accompanied by a delicious local Merlot.
Via dei Gorini 2.
Tel: (091) 923 52 19.
Closed: Sun & Aug.

SPORT AND LEISURE

Monte Tamaro

Take the cable car to the top of the mountain to this popular adventure park, with hiking and biking trails, an acrobatic course (five levels from children to expert), and Ticino's longest summer bobsleigh run.
Tel: (091) 946 23 03.
www.montetamaro.ch.
Open: July & Aug 8.30am–6pm; Apr–June & Sept–early Nov 8.30am–5pm.

Index

Acknowledgements

Teresa Fisher would like to thank Switzerland Tourism (*www.myswitzerland.com*), the Switzerland Travel Centre (*tel: 0800 100 200 30*) and Emmanuel Vermot for their help in the preparation of this book.

Thomas Cook Publishing wishes to thank CHRISTOF SONDEREGGER for the photographs in this book, to whom the copyright belongs, except for the following images:

DREAMSTIME C Elmanoli 1; S Brunett; 13; Astra490 77; I Lumb 131

For CAMBRIDGE PUBLISHING MANAGEMENT LTD:
Project editor: Diane Teillol
Typesetter: Trevor Double
Proofreader: Frances Darby
Indexer: Karolin Thomas

SEND YOUR THOUGHTS TO
BOOKS@THOMASCOOK.COM

We're committed to providing the very best up-to-date information in our travel guides and constantly strive to make them as useful as they can be. You can help us to improve future editions by letting us have your feedback. If you've made a wonderful discovery on your travels that we don't already feature, if you'd like to inform us about recent changes to anything that we do include, or if you simply want to let us know your thoughts about this guidebook and how we can make it even better – we'd love to hear from you.

Send us ideas, discoveries and recommendations today and then look out for your valuable input in the next edition of this title.

Emails to the above address, or letters to Travellers Series Editor, Thomas Cook Publishing, PO Box 227, Coningsby Road, Peterborough PE3 8SB, UK.

Please don't forget to let us know which title your feedback refers to!